BLACK
NONFICTION BOOKS,
THEIR AUTHORS,
AND THEIR PUBLISHERS

About the Author

Harry B. Dunbar is a memoirist and the author of *A Brother Like Me: A Memoir*, published in 1995 under his own imprint. He is a reviewer and annotator of books by and about black people. His online newsletter "Dunbar on Black Books" has been published monthly on the Internet since November 1997 and on his own domain since June 2000. He is a bibliographer specializing in nonfiction books by and about black people in the United States and has compiled a bibliography which is a representative sampling of these books published in the last five years of the twentieth century. He is a student of the history of the publishing of black nonfiction books.

Harry B. Dunbar has been a member of Alpha Phi Alpha Fraternity, Inc., for over fifty-two years and sits on its Historical Commission. He contributed the epilogue to the seventeenth and final edition of *The History of Alpha Phi Alpha: A Development in College Life*, by Charles H. Wesley, which was published in 2000. The original edition was published in 1929.

Harry B. Dunbar, chairman of the Publications Committee of Alpha Phi Alpha Fraternity during the presidency of Adrian L. Wallace, from 1997 to 2001, is the recipient of the Alpha Phi Alpha Meritorious Service Award. *Black Nonfiction Books, Their Authors, and Their Publishers: A History, a Bibliography, and a Memoir* is the result of a blending of these interests and experiences.

BLACK
NONFICTION BOOKS,
THEIR AUTHORS,
AND THEIR PUBLISHERS

A HISTORY,
A BIBLIOGRAPHY,
AND A MEMOIR

Harry B. Dunbar

Foreword by Julius E. Thompson

QUEENHYTE PUBLISHERS

THIS IS A QUEENHYTE BOOK

Copyright © 2002 by Harry B. Dunbar. All rights reserved under International and Pan-American Copyright Conventions. Published in the United States by Queenhyte Publishers, 119 Rockland Center, Ste. 320, Nanuet, NY 10954-2968.

Design and composition by C+S GOTTFRIED.
Index by IndexEmpire Indexing Services.

ISBN 0-9643654-1-3

LIBRARY OF CONGRESS CATALOGING-IN-PUBLICATION DATA

Dunbar, Harry B.
    Black Nonfiction Books, Their Authors, and Their Publishers / by
    Harry B. Dunbar - 1st ed.
                    p. ; cm
    Includes index.
    ISBN 0-9643654-1-3

TABLE OF CONTENTS

*This book is dedicated
to my wife Charlene
and to my daughter Nona Louise.*

FOREWORD

Julius E. Thompson

Harry B. Dunbar's *Black Nonfiction Books, Their Authors, and Their Publishers: A History, A Bibliography, and A Memoir* is an excellent study which illustrates the nature of publishing on and about African Americans in this nation from the 1700s to the year 2000. The author has two goals. The first is to give a thorough summary and historical analysis of the printing of nonfiction books produced in America by and/or about black people. The second is to offer readers a sense of the author's own experiences, perspectives, and attitudes about this body of work. Thus, Dunbar's sweep of the history of black nonfiction publishing draws upon three of his strengths to focus attention on the development of black publishing: he uses his skills as a bibliographer, as a memoirist, and as a bibliophile to give contemporary readers a greater understanding of and historical feel for nonfiction books produced across three hundred years by or about African-American subjects.

Dunbar captures the complexity of nonfiction publishing in the black U.S. world. He carries readers from the slavery experience period, when the first recorded black publications began to

appear, to the twentieth century, the high point of black publishing activities. Along the way, the efforts of the giant forerun-
ners among black publishers are noted, including the work of the
black church and fraternal organizations, black businesses, and
especially the black press and black educational institutions. He
also includes key individuals and the organizations with which
they were associated, such as Carter G. Woodson and the Associated Publishers in Washington, D.C.; Charles H. Wesley and
Howard University Press; Alain Locke and the Associates in
Negro Folk Education; and Foundation Publishers, an in-house
subsidiary of Alpha Phi Alpha Fraternity, Inc., and publisher of
Charles H. Wesley's history of the fraternity. As an important
element in black publishing activity Dunbar adds to this impres-
sive list the work of William E. B. Du Bois, both as author of *The
Souls of Black Folk,* one of the greatest books by a black American
author, and as writer, publisher, and editor of *The Crisis Magazine,*
the official organ of the NAACP. The career and work of Dudley Randall and Broadside Press (established in 1965 in Detroit)
are also highlighted. Randall was able to publish over four hundred writers in his press devoted to poetry, anthologies, and
other creative works. Also of importance has been John H. Johnson's Johnson Publishing Company of Chicago, creator of *Ebony*
and *Jet* magazines and publisher of many books on the black
experience in America. A dozen other major black publishing
firms of the last century are also noted, as well as nonfiction titles
produced by mainstream white publishers and the body of work
contributed to the field by self-published blacks with their own
private publishing outlets.

    In essence, Dunbar captures the complex nature of black
publishing across three hundred years. He has a special interest
in works which reflect upon the universal experience of blacks
and which have some real meaning in relation to his own personal story (i.e., the nature of being black in a racist society and

of overcoming the concomitant limitations placed on the human spirit and outlook by that society). He finds an especially significant place among black nonfiction works for autobiographies and biographies written by, or on, African-American figures. On his list of the most outstanding books produced by blacks in the twentieth century, he reserves an especially high ranking for several works of this genre.

Harry B. Dunbar's book offers readers the opportunity to reflect upon several hundred years of the production of nonfiction books on blacks in America. It focuses special attention on the efforts of black intellectuals to define the African-American experience and to seek a greater understanding of the past, as it relates to the present and may, indeed, influence the future. It also offers encouragement to young and old alike to take up the pen and discover the rewards for writing for oneself, thus contributing to the ageless quest for human understanding while promoting equality, liberty, and human advancement.

This well-documented book is one that will be an invaluable tool for researchers seeking information about the history and development of the publishing of nonfiction books by and about blacks in America.

ACKNOWLEDGMENTS

I am indebted to many people for the help that enabled me to write this book. My wife Charlene is first among them. Her patience, love, and understanding have been abundant over the forty-seven years of our marriage and my authoring of this second book in the last six years. My sister Louise Dunbar Robbins served as my editor. She has had extensive experience in teaching expository writing at the undergraduate as well as the graduate level at various colleges. Those who don't know what an expert on readability can do for an author need only to have seen the manuscript for this book before she counseled me. When I said to one of her children that she is an excellent editor, that young lady said to me, "Ma is an inveterate nitpicker."

My daughter Nona Louise merits acknowledgment as a ready adviser when consulted. Her more than twenty years as an editor for one of the largest-circulation, English-language periodicals in the world has in more than a few instances been brought to bear on matters on which I have consulted her.

Adrian Wallace, immediate past president of Alpha Phi Alpha Fraternity, Inc., has had a significant influence on me in the writing of this book. His teaming me with outstanding scholars, notably Thomas D. Pawley III, Julius E. Thompson, and

Robert L. Harris, Jr., among others, on an Alpha Phi Alpha Fraternity project has given me a unique perspective on the fraternity's role in the history of the publication of nonfiction books in America.

PART ONE

A Black Book Canon

A Legacy from the Nineteenth Century

Chapter 1

A Bibliomemoirist's Musings

Why this book about this genre? This book is conceived to serve two purposes. The first is to sketch the history of the publication of nonfiction books by and about black people in the United States. The second is to share with my paper-and-ink-book readers some of the opinions, insights, and ideas about black nonfiction books that I have shared with my cyberspace audience. As a book reviewer and annotator of books by and about black people for a weekly newspaper I have become aware that many persons who read my column about black books have no access at all to my online column, "Dunbar on Black Books" (www.queenhyte. com/dobb). These persons, God love them, do buy and read books. I hope they read this one.

As a bibliographer who is a memoirist, my reading of books seeds my memoirs. In the paper-and-ink mode, the bibliomemoir best accommodates my interests as bibliographer, bibliophile, and memoirist. Further, as a literary narcissist who looks in the stream of literature to see his reflection, the bibliomemoir is my genre of choice. It best enables me to insinuate myself into the company and the thought of the likes of W. E. B. Du Bois and of Stephen L. Carter, to mention but two. I have always lived in that region of blue sky and wandering shadows that Du Bois said some of us inhabit. It is from this perspective that I share with my readers reviews of some of the works in the 907-book "Dunbar Black Book Bibliography." My readers from cyberspace will find that the historical matter on the afroimprint covers new ground.

A NINETEENTH-CENTURY BIBLIOGRAPHER'S LEGACY

In 1976, Robert L. Harris, Jr., associate professor of African American History and director of the Africana Studies and Research Center at Cornell University, called attention to, and threw light on, the most comprehensive bibliography of books by and about black people that had been produced in this country in 1900 and on Daniel Murray, its compiler.* Harris's study, published during this nation's bicentennial year, served to spotlight Daniel Murray and his role in conceptualizing a black encyclopedia, which idea had been generally associated almost exclusively with W. E. B. Du Bois. Harris's study informs us that Daniel Murray had labored for more than twenty-five years on a black encyclopedia and that, working independently, he had invited and had acceptance by many eminent black intellectuals to join the editorial staff of "Murray's Encyclopedia."

The encyclopedia's major feature, as conceived by Murray was to be twenty-five thousand biographical sketches of prominent men and women of color, as well as those whites who had

---

*Robert L. Harris, Jr., "Daniel Murray and the Encyclopedia of the Colored Race," *Phylon,* September 1976.

promoted the cause of justice. Further, the Harris study tells us, editor-in-chief Murray estimated that about forty thousand entries culled from more than a million books would complete the text. The cost of pulling this publication together was very high and not within the means of Murray. Suggestions from Du Bois that Murray publish some of his material in *The Crisis Magazine* as a way of publicizing the work and of stimulating public interest and securing assistance for printing the encyclopedia fell on deaf ears. Murray refused to publish the work piecemeal. As a consequence, Harris points out, "Murray's dogged determination to have his entire enterprise appear at once probably prevented its publication."

Murray, however, was to become the twentieth century's primary bibliographer of books by and about black people. In 1871 he had been hired by Ainsworth Rand Spofford, the Librarian of Congress, as his personal assistant. In 1899, Herbert Putnam, Spofford's successor, asked Murray to compile a collection of books and pamphlets by black authors for an exhibition of "Negro Authors" at the Paris Exposition of 1900. Murray published a preliminary list of titles in 1900, appealing to the public for donations of listed works, as well as suggested additions. Five hundred of these books were exhibited at the Paris Exposition. Within several months, his list grew to eleven hundred titles.

The collection became the core of the Library of Congress's "Colored Authors' Collection." In 1926, the year following Murray's death, the Library received a bequest of 1148 books and pamphlets that Murray had privately assembled. These volumes were added to the Colored Authors' Collection and were later integrated with the general collections of the Library, with many duplicates being transferred to Howard University. Twenty-two volumes of bound pamphlets were transferred to the Rare Books and Special Collections Division. These volumes form the current Daniel A. P. Murray Pamphlet Collection.

THE AUTOAFROIMPRINT: A
TWENTIETH-CENTURY PHOENIX

In ancient mythology there are Egyptian, Roman, and Chinese legends about the phoenix, a beautiful lone bird which lived in the Arabian desert for over five hundred years and then consumed itself in fire, rising renewed from the ashes to start another long life. The expression "rising phoenixlike from the ashes" has come to symbolize something rebuilt after it had been destroyed. The "autoafroimprint" is a twentieth-century incarnation of the phoenix. Whether it has re-created itself after it had been destroyed or whether it has been alive all along and now manifests itself after not having been seen for a long time is a matter for debate. What is clear is that it is alive and well.

As conceived by this writer, an "afroimprint" is any book which is by or about black people and/or has issues which impact on us, irrespective of who the author may be. To use the paradigm of W. Paul Coates, the publisher of Black Classic Press in Baltimore, any book written by a black person, even one about butterflies, is a black book. By our definition then, any book published at any time by or about black people or with issues which impact on us in this country is an afroimprint. These books may be written by persons of any race, but if published by a publishing house not controlled by blacks, they are afroimprints. An exemplar: *Souls of Black Folk,* by W. E. B. Du Bois (A. C. McClurg & Co., 1903).*

On the other hand, a book that, phoenixlike, created itself in the sense that it was written by a black and published under his or her control is an "autoafroimprint." Books published by vanity presses are excluded since control of those presses is not in the hands of black people. An example of an autoafroimprint is *The*

---

*The Dunbar Black Book Bibliography (DBBB), in Part 2, began as a resource list of nonfiction books by or about blacks, with notations of where I found the citations. By 1997 or so I decided to convert the list to bibliographic format.

History of the Negro Church, by Carter G. Woodson (Associated Publishers, 1921).

The "neo-autoafroimprint" is a book published after 1990 by a publishing house under black control. Some neo-autoafroimprints, due to their professional quality and the lack of information regarding their "genealogy," are mistakenly considered afroimprints. An example: *A Brother Like Me: A Memoir,* by Harry B. Dunbar (Queenhyte Publishers, 1995).

CHAPTER 2

AFRICAN-AMERICAN IMPRINTS IN THE EIGHTEENTH AND NINETEENTH CENTURIES

A Historical Sketch

Joan Potter and Constance Claytor, in their book *African American Firsts* (Pinto Press, 1994), include three African-American authors of published works dating from the eighteenth century which bear mention here, in that they are unequivocal autoafroimprints. Potter and Claytor point to these three authors respectively as (1) the first African American to write a poem that was later published, (2) the first African American to write prose that was published, and (3) the first African-American man to write a poem that was published. I have not documented any of the three.

As Potter and Claytor tell it, Lucy Terry, author of the first published poem by an African American, came to America on a slave ship and was brought to Deerfield, Massachusetts, when she was about five years old. When she was sixteen years of age, she wrote a poem about a battle between Native Americans and whites at The Bars, an area outside of Deerfield. Titled "Bars Fight," Terry wrote it in 1746, but it was not published until 1893. This poem was Terry's only published work. A talented storyteller, at age twenty she married Abijah Prince, and they settled in Vermont where they raised six children. Two of their sons fought in the American Revolution. Terry, who lived to be ninety-one, was an ardent fighter for equal rights for her family.

The first published prose written by an African American, as reported by Potter and Claytor, is an autobiographical piece titled *A Narrative of the Uncommon Sufferings and Surprising Deliverance of Briton Hammon, a Negro Man.* Potter and Claytor tell us that it is unclear whether Hammon was a servant or a slave. In the narrative he relates how, with permission from his master, given in 1747, he sailed from his Massachusetts home on a sloop headed to the islands of the West Indies. As he relates it, his ship was caught on a reef on the return voyage. He was captured by Native Americans, escaped, and eventually reached England. There he signed on a ship headed for Boston. He discovered, to his delight, Potter and Claytor tell us, that by coincidence, his master was on the ship. The narrative was published as a 14-page pamphlet in Boston in 1760.

The evolution of the imprints under which the early black nonfiction books were published is difficult to trace and document. I have been unable to track the original Briton Hammon document and determine its publisher, but did find a bibliographical reference to the pamphlet in the catalog of the New York Public Library, indicating that a reprint of the pamphlet is in its Schomburg Collection. The imprint for the reprint of this document, published in 1972, bears the notation: "Mandeln. Kraus Reprint." In this citation the author's name is given as "Briton Hamman." Interestingly, the title of the document in the Schomburg Collection fills in gaps. In this source, the pamphlet is entitled *Narrative of the Uncommon Sufferings and Surprizing Deliverance of Briton Hamman A Negro-Man Servant to General Winslow, of Marshfield, in New-England: Who returned to Boston, after having been absent almost thirteen years.*

In addition to being intrigued by Briton Hammon's odyssey, I wonder why he went through the travail that he did to return to bondage after thirteen years of freedom, if indeed he had been a slave. It would be interesting to know how this resourceful man got his work published. As enterprising as he seems to have been, it has to be a fascinating story.

There are fully documentable eighteenth-century publishing achievements which bear mention here. One relates to Phillis Wheatley, who was born in Africa around 1753 and arrived in Boston on a slave ship when she was about eight years of age. In Boston she was bought by a wealthy tailor and merchant named John Wheatley. The Wheatley family educated her and encouraged the development of her talent for writing poetry. When she was a teenager, she wrote an elegy on the death of Rev. George Whitefield, a noted evangelist. It was published in 1770. Two years later the Wheatleys tried to have a volume of Phillis's poems published but prospective publishers would not believe that she was the author. The solution that was found was to have a group of eighteen prominent Bostonians question her and write a two-paragraph introduction attesting to her ability. Accompanied by her master's son, she traveled to England and was introduced to a number of prominent citizens. Her book, *Poems on Various Subjects, Religious and Moral,* was published there in 1773. This book is reported to be the first book of writings of any kind to be published by an African American.

AUTOAFROIMPRINTS, 1800–1899

I am indebted to Robert Fleming (*The African American Writer's Handbook*) for a citation of African-American books published in this country in the eighteenth and nineteenth centuries. These afroimprints, encompassing fiction, nonfiction, and poetry, certainly form the foundation on which the tradition of nonfiction black book publishing was built in the twentieth century. The writings of Benjamin Banneker, William Wells Brown, Charles W. Chesnutt, Alexander Crummell, Martin Delany, Frederick Douglass, Paul Laurence Dunbar, Olaudah Equino, T. Thomas Fortune, Frances E. W. Harper, Mary Prince, Phillis Wheatley, and Harriet Wilson are literal and figurative volumes still on the twenty-first-century bookshelf.

Autoafroimprints predate the twentieth century. An ongoing project of the Library at the University of North Carolina at Chapel Hill provides good documentation on the subject. The project, called "Documenting the American South" (DAS) is compiling a bibliography titled "The Church in the Southern Black Community." A study of the imprints that are represented in this work provides ample documentation of the fact that the black church and its several denominations had established autoafroimprints which were producing nonfiction books before the twentieth century dawned.

For example, DAS lists a 79-page book, *The Evangelical Catechism, or a Plain and Easy System of the Principal Doctrines and Duties of the Christian Religion, Adapted to the Use of Sabbath Schools and Families with a New Method of Instructing Those Who Cannot Read.* This book, by John Mines, was published in 1821 by N. Pollard. I believe that both Mines and Pollard were black and that this book qualifies as an autoafroimprint. Also cited is *Biography of Rev. David Smith of the A.M.E. Church: Being a Complete History, Embracing over Sixty Years' Labor in the Advancement of the Redeemer's Kingdom on Earth,* by David Smith. This book, printed at the Xenia Gazette office in Xenia,

Ohio, in 1881 is unquestionably an autoafroimprint. The A.M.E. Publishing House, with a publication under the date of 1897, is another pre-twentieth-century autoafroimprint. The DAS bibliography enables us to make the claim that Atlanta University had a publishing arm in 1898.* Moreover, Du Bois' *The Negro Church: Report of a Social Study Made under the Direction of Atlanta University, Together with the Proceedings of the Eighth Conference for the Study of the Negro Problem*, published by the Atlanta University Press, in 1903, figures in this bibliography. His *Souls of Black Folk*, brought out by A. C. McClurg and Company, also in 1903, is included. In any event, afroimprints and autoafroimprints can be said to have provided the wind under the wings of the twentieth-century incarnation of the phoenix.

The DAS bibliography documents the fact that mainstream publishers brought out afroimprints before 1901. Such works under the following years and imprints are part of this bibliography: G. Putnam's Sons, 1875; J. B. Lippencott [*sic*] Company, 1888; and The John Hopkins Press, 1896. There are a number of afroimprints and highly probable autoafroimprints with publication years from 1822 to 1921 in this bibliography.

On the basis of the DAS bibliography I feel I can say that nonfiction books by and about African Americans had gained a place in the publishing firmament during the nineteenth century, largely through the initiatives of the several denominations of the black church. Also, evidences of black college and/or university publishing enterprises began to manifest themselves at the turn of the century.

It is known that Atlanta University Press had published before the turn of the century. While it is not clear whether there

---

*The following is evidence that Atlanta University had a press before the turn of the century: "Du Bois, W. E. B. 'Some Efforts of American Negroes for Their Own Social Betterment. Report of an Investigation under the Direction of Atlanta University.' Atlanta, Ga.: Atlanta University Press, 1898. 66 p."

was a connection to Wilberforce University in Xenia, Ohio, the aforementioned 1881 biography of Rev. David Smith of the African Methodist Episcopal (A.M.E.) Church may have been related to the university. (The biography of Rev. David Smith might better have been titled an autobiography.) The Aldine Press, also seated in Xenia, Ohio, and which in 1906 brought out Horace Talbert's *The Sons of Allen,* may also have had some connection with this A.M.E. institution. Finally, the DAS bibliography permits me to conclude that in 1908 at the latest, Hampton Institute had a book publishing enterprise which brought out a history of African Methodism in Virginia.

Ann Plato

Not much is known about Ann Plato, the first African American to publish a book of essays. She was born in Hartford, Connecticut about 1820. From approximately the age of fifteen she was a teacher of children. Her book, entitled *Essays: Including Biographies and Miscellaneous Pieces, In Prose and Poetry,* was published in 1841. Reportedly the second book published by a black woman, it contained sixteen essays and twenty poems.

William Wells Brown

William Wells Brown's novel *Clotel, or The President's Daughter: A Narrative of Slave Life in the United States,* was first published in London in 1853. It is the story of a child born to President Thomas Jefferson's African-American housekeeper. It was published in the United States in 1864 with a different title: *Clotelle: A Tale of the Southern States or a Leap for Freedom,* which makes no reference to the president. Brown had been a slave who escaped and fled north. He wrote about the evils of slavery in his books and plays, notably in his *Narrative of William Wells Brown: A Fugitive Slave* (1847). He lectured widely on slavery here and abroad.

CHAPTER 3

THE TWENTIETH-CENTURY BLACK NONFICTION BOOK

A Contemporary Bibliographer's Perspective

AFROIMPRINTS, 1901–1937

From our twenty-first-century vantage point I see the black non-fiction book phoenix as a manifestation of the Chinese genus of its species. It is a species that dates back to the mid-1700s and is flourishing today. Whether viewed solely through the prism of the afroimprint, through that of the autoafroimprint, or through both prisms, the black nonfiction book phoenix manifests the trait symbolized by the Chinese species: longevity.

The twentieth-century incarnation of the nonfiction afroimprint phoenix, seen here for the first time in 1901, sprang from the hand of Booker T. Washington and the Doubleday imprint under the title *Up from Slavery.* (The Library of Congress online catalog has the following entry: "*An autobiography: The story of my life and work* by Booker T. Washington . . . with an introduction by Dr. J. L. M. Curry. Rev. ed. Toronto, Ont., Naperville, Ill., etc.: J. L. Nichols & Co. [c.1901].") This is a 423-page illustrated volume. Unlike the phoenix described by Pliny of ancient Rome, which existed only one at a time on earth, the phoenix of 1901 was replicated in 1907. Again from the hand of Washington, the Library of Congress online catalog shows "*Frederick Douglass,* by Booker T. Washington, Philadelphia, London, G.W. Jacobs & company [1907]."

Daisy Anderson and *From Slavery to Affluence*

In 1927, the remarkable memoir of an ex-slave came into print. Its existence calls to mind the comment attributed to Lyman Bryson that the wonder of a woman preacher is not that she doesn't do it well, but that she does it at all. The memoir of Robert Anderson, a former slave and Union soldier, merits our attention here.

Entitled *From Slavery to Affluence,* it was written and published by his wife Daisy Anderson. This book bears five copyright years: 1927, 1967, 1986, 1995, and 1997. It was published in Steamboat Springs, Colorado, and bears all the earmarks of the selfpublished work that it is. It is a masterful tribute paid by a wife to a beloved husband. Further, it is the story of a most unlikely husband and wife team. It is a significant contribution to the history of the autoafroimprint.

Mrs. Anderson, née Daisy Graham, was twenty-one years of age when she married Robert Anderson in Forest City, Arkansas,

in 1922. He was seventy-nine. Born into slavery in Green County, Kentucky, on March 1, 1843, he fled the flax and hemp plantation in Kentucky during the waning days of the Civil War in
1865 and joined the Union Army, according to his widow's obit-
uary, which was published in the *New York Times* in 1998. After his
discharge in 1867 he attempted several unsuccessful farming ventures. He then acquired a 2000-acre homestead in Nebraska and
became wealthy. In 1922 when he came to Forest City, Arkansas,
to visit his brother, he was not only wealthy but lonely. There, a
matchmaking preacher introduced him to Daisy Graham. We are
told that he captivated "Miss Daisy" with his talk about his
experiences as a slave, soldier, and gentleman farmer. Thirty days
after being introduced, their May–December marriage took
place. In 1927, Daisy Anderson turned the stories that her husband had told her into a book about his life and published the
book herself. She described their marriage, which ended in 1930
when her husband was killed in an automobile accident, as an
eight-year honeymoon.

The story is that, spoiled by her late husband's generosity,
Daisy Anderson became a spendthrift and during the Great
Depression lost the holdings that he had left to her. She became
a lecturer in her later years and spent her life working for racial
harmony and keeping the memory of her late husband alive. She
became a minor celebrity, was introduced to Pope John Paul in
1993, and in 1997 presented a copy of her book to President
Clinton.

After reading the book, I was left with the thought that no
publisher would have had the ingenuity, the capacity, or the
desire to arrange an audience with the pope or a meeting with the
president of the United States at which to present him with a
copy of this book. Daisy Anderson, the irrepressible autoafroimprint manager, was able to do for her book what the biggest publishing house could not or would not have done. Daisy Ander-

son died at age ninety-seven in Denver, Colorado, on September 19, 1998.

The development of several significant autoafroimprints after World War I contributed substantially to the quality and vigor of the autoafroimprint output. In 1921 Carter G. Woodson founded Associated Publishers in Washington, D.C. This imprint published his *The History of the Negro Church* in that year. In 1929 Howard University Press published the first edition of *The History of Alpha Phi Alpha: A Development in College Life* by Dr. Charles H. Wesley, then the historian of Alpha Phi Alpha Fraternity, Inc.

1936–1945

In the 1930s Alain Locke of Howard University headed Associates in Negro Folk Education, which published Ralph Bunche's *A World View of Race*, in 1936, and Sterling Brown's *The Negro in American Fiction*, in 1937.

Since 1935, Foundation Publishers, an in-house subsidiary of Alpha Phi Alpha Fraternity, Inc., has published seventeen editions of its history. The seventeenth edition, updated by Dr. Robert L. Harris, the fraternity historian, was published in 2000 and includes an epilogue in tribute to Dr. Wesley by this author. I am indebted to Dr. Thomas D. Pawley III, a former national historian of Alpha Phi Alpha, for an insight into this autoafroimprint and its place on the roster of black nonfiction publishing initiatives.

From Pawley's research we learn that at some time between 1929 and 1935, when Alpha Phi Alpha was ready to bring out the second edition of its history, the Howard University Press was no longer operating. The demise of this autoafroimprint was a substantial blow to the publication of black nonfiction books because, Pawley says, "the Howard University Press . . . with the Associate Publishers of the Association for the Study of Negro

Life and History were probably the two most important agencies for publishing works of African-American scholars."

An insight into the history of the Howard University Press is obtained from a document entitled "The Development of the Howard University Publishing Program," by Clifford L. Muse, Jr., Ph.D. From this document which is in the University Archives, we learn that the university's Industrial Department became the unofficial university press in 1883 and that the first publication by the office was titled "The University Reporter." The imprint "Howard University Press" first appeared in 1892 in a publication featuring the memorial address honoring Dr. George Burrell Cheever and delivered by Henry Theodore Cheever. The Howard University Press became an official unit of the university when the board of trustees passed an enabling resolution on February 7, 1919. On October 25, 1932, the press was abolished, the university printing office closed, and the equipment sold. University publications were produced by commercial printers. In 1959 the Howard University Press was reestablished but existed in name only until 1972 when it launched a true publishing program of diverse works.

By the establishment of Foundation Publishers, it was the intention of Alpha Phi Alpha Fraternity to encourage scholarly activity within the fraternity by publishing books written by members. Foundation Publishers was established at Howard University by eight members of the fraternity, four of whom were members of the faculty there. In addition to the *History*, other books were published under this imprint, whose books Pawley sees as furthering the aim of the imprint as conceived by Wesley.

Those books were (1) *The Attitude of the Southern Press toward Negro Suffrage*, by Rayford W. Logan, (2) *The Convention Address of the General President 1933–1940*, by Charles H. Wesley, and (3) *Henry Arthur Callis: Life and Legacy*, by Charles H. Wesley, 1977. The eight incorporators who were also the first directors and trustees of the publishing corporation included Rayford W. Logan, professor of history at Atlanta University and Howard University; Howard Long, associate superintendent of the public schools of the District of Columbia, later dean of Wilberforce Unversity and Central State College, in Ohio; Walter F. Jerrick of Philadelphia; Sydney Brown, an attorney; Dwight O. W. Holmes, dean of the Graduate School at Howard University and later president of Morgan State College; H. Council Trenholm, president of Alabama State College; Charles H. Wesley, head of the Department of History at Howard University and later president of Wilberforce University and of Central State University, in Ohio; and Charles H. Thompson, professor of education, Howard University, and editor of *The Journal of Negro Education.*

THE AUTOAFROIMPRINT, 1936–1978

The autoafroimprint, as it emerged in the first quarter of the twentieth century, rested on four sturdy pillars: W. E. B. Du Bois and the Atlanta University Press; Carter G. Woodson and The Association for the Study of Negro Life and History, Inc.; Alain Locke and The Associates in Negro Folk Education; and Charles H. Wesley and Foundation Publishers. The work of these men in many instances remains in print today under the aegis of these imprints.

In 1936, Franklin D. Roosevelt was reelected president of the United States. In 1936, Jesse Owens won four gold medals in the Olympics held in Berlin. In 1936, twenty thousand spectators gathered in Owensboro, Kentucky, to witness the last public hanging, at which Rainey Bethea, a black murderer, was put to death. Also in 1936, on March 10, an unheralded event took place in Washington, D.C. A certificate of incorporation for Foundation Publishers of Alpha Phi Alpha Fraternity, Inc., was filed in the District of Columbia. This historic action brought another autoafroimprint online to complement the already-existing Atlanta University Press, The Associates in Negro Folk Education, and The Association for the Study of Negro Life and History, Inc.

In 1935, before its incorporation, Foundation Publishers brought out the above-mentioned volume by Charles H. Wesley. In 1936, The Associates in Negro Folk Education published the above-mentioned *A World View of Race*, by Ralph J. Bunche, a young Howard University professor, later to become a major figure in the United Nations. That year it also published *The Negro and His Music*, by Alain Locke. The Association for the Study of Negro Life and History, Inc., published *The African Background Outlined, or Handbook for the Study of the Negro*. Here I make the case that the year 1936 marks the firming up of a black scholarly publishing community which manifested, and continues to manifest, the highest standards of scholarship. This community of scholars, while clustered around Washington, D.C., and Howard University, extended to Atlanta and Atlanta University.

While Fisk University was a center of scholarly activity from the late nineteenth century with published scholars on its faculty, it does not appear to have had its own press. The online catalog of the Library of Congress shows that the Department of Publicity of Fisk University published a 35-page book on James Weldon Johnson. The date of the publication is uncertain, since the catalog entry has 1941 with a question mark following.

In any event, this scholarly publishing community holds its own even today when many of the men and women who are its natural members have been drawn into the wider scholarly community. I have an inclination to include their works under the rubric of autoafroimprints.

During the thirty-year period from 1939 to 1969 the members of the autoafroimprint brain trust distinguished themselves in American letters, in academia, in scholarship, in government, and in every domain where educated men and women are revered. During this period they began to win distinguished places in these aforementioned fields beyond the confines of what had heretofore been narrow, race-defined compartments. In many ways this validated them and the institutions from which they were recruited. The men who were prominent in the creation of the first autoafroimprint ventures are eminent examples. Many of them may be said to have been the implements in the machine shops that turned out the finely tooled scholars who were prepared to move into positions of leadership when affirmative action became the order of the day.

THE NEW ERA AUTOAFROIMPRINTS

In 1999 I began to pay closer attention to a phenomenon that I had not seen in its own context: nonfiction books written, published, and promoted by black authors. In March 1999 in an essay entitled "Black Books under the Radar," published in my online periodical "Dunbar on Black Books," I likened most books published by black authors to small airplanes which fly in the airspace at levels which are not tracked by radar devices. No flight plans (i.e., prepublication forecasts) are filed for them in the industry. The industry air control towers (i.e., the reviewers) do not herald, much less monitor, them. The best-seller lists do not plot their cruising altitudes or provide relevant information about them.

I noted that many of these aircraft were not airworthy and were a menace to aviation. That is, many of them bear telltale indices of corner cutting in their editing, design, and technical features. However, it is my observation that there are also some eminently commendable nonfiction books being produced by some new imprints without track records. I detected a certain vigor in the under-the-radar black book environment, fueled by a coterie of black micropublishing entrepreneurs who are bringing out nonfiction books of good to excellent quality.

The African American Online Writers Guild (AAOWG), which claims to be the largest community of black writers on the Internet, took note of the increasing number of self-published books by black "literary entrepreneurs."* *Black Issues Book Review* (BIBR) began a regular column on the subject. "Dunbar on Black Books" and Queenhyte Publishers began to look at the phenomenon, at some of the men and women who are driving it, and at the imprints which are involved. "Dunbar on Black Books" and Queenhyte Publishers took great interest in the number of these books by and about blacks which belong to the nonfiction canon. We were impressed and encouraged by the obvious quality of the imprints under which these books are being published. Those persons who are the backbone of the under-the-radar black book community are of particular interest to us. This black book community is developing into a vital one and is even ushering some of its members into the mainstream of American book publishing.

In the October 1997 issue of "Dunbar on Black Books" online, I observed that while it is part of conventional wisdom that books by and about blacks were experiencing a surge in popularity that was of recent vintage, the evidence was that it dated from an earlier era. True, the black Mother-Daughter Book Club, founded in 1991 in New York, was the focus of a feature article in the *New York Times* in July 1997. A look into the subject showed that the surge in interest in black books goes back at least to the 1960s.

In a report titled "Books on Negroes Gaining in Sales," Theodore Jones (*New York Times,* December 14, 1963) observed that the quest of blacks for civil rights and the emergence of independent African nations created a growing demand in

---

*In 2001, AAOWG became the Black Writers Alliance.

Harlem for books on Negro and African history. This demand appears to have stimulated the growth of at least two Harlem concerns specializing in distributing literature on black and African culture and affairs.

In 1963, when Jones was writing, The Negro Book Club had grown to four thousand members after a start in 1960 with about a thousand members. With headquarters on 85th Street, the club had three full-time employees and fifty part-time field representatives. In addition, it had a hundred displays in stores throughout the New York metropolitan area. Most of the club members lived in Harlem, the president told the *Times* reporter. Further, he added, word-of-mouth communication had resulted in new club memberships from as far away as Philadelphia and Washington. The club was founded because similar organizations were not meeting the need for books on Negro history and African life.

Another book group which credited its success to the demand for Negro literature was the Dunbar Book Company. It was owned and operated by two blacks in their late twenties and was started in 1963 as a mail-order company and then expanded, opening a bookstore on 125th Street.

Clearly, these developments were replicated, and other book-related activities were implemented in other locations throughout the nation, and together explain the phenomenon which we are witnessing today in the black book industry. Where are black books today in the context of the entire publishing industry? A report in *Publishers Weekly* (September 15, 1997) cites Target Market News, a Chicago research firm specializing in the African-American market, as the source of the information that from 1993 to 1996, the amount that black households spent on books grew to $261 million from $178 million. Publishers and booksellers are not unmindful of this. Further, the president of Target Market News is quoted as saying that this "Terry McMillan effect" of the last three years is not going to slow down anytime soon.

From the 1960s onward several new black book publishing ventures were founded and they launched a new generation of top-notch nonfiction authors. A few of them merit our attention here.

Without a doubt, Broadside Press is the primordial new era autoafroimprint. The story of this publishing venture and of its remarkable founder documents this assertion. In *Dudley Randall, Broadside Press, and the Black Arts Movement in Detroit, 1960–1995* (McFarland & Company, 1999), Julius E. Thompson has provided ample proof. Dr. Thompson, director of the Black Studies Program and associate professor of history at the University of Missouri, in Columbia, has brought impeccable scholarship, searching insight, and credible synthesis to his study of Dudley Randall, of Broadside Press, and of the Black Arts Movement in Detroit. Thompson's book serves as a window on the man, the press, and the movement that sparked the careers of so many black authors.

We get a clear picture of Dudley Randall, who as both a writer and a publisher was, to use Thompson's term, the "major role" figure for the second Renaissance, the Black Arts Movement of the 1960s and 1970s. To the mind of this reviewer, it is no exaggeration to see Dudley Randall's role not only as the prime catalyst in the Black Arts Movement in Detroit in the 1960s and 1970s but also as the progenitor of the black book surge that we are seeing today.

Dudley Randall was born in 1914 in Washington, D.C., where his mother was a teacher. His father was a teacher, a school principal, and a congregational minister. When Randall was five or six years of age, the family moved to East St. Louis, Illinois, where his father had accepted a position with the YMCA. After a year in East St. Louis, the Randall family moved to Detroit in 1921. Dudley attended public elementary schools there. In 1926 he entered Eastern High School. It was there, in 1927, at age thirteen, that Dudley Randall's apprenticeship to poetry began when one of his sonnets was selected as a first-prize winner for publication on the "Young Poet's Page" of the *Detroit Free Press*. Two years after graduating from high school in 1930 during the Great Depression, Randall got his first full-time job in the Ford River Rouge plant.

From 1932 to 1935 he worked in the Ford plant and continued to study and write poetry at home. As late as 1939, when he was twenty-five years of age, he was still unpublished, and as Thompson observes, his work remained largely hidden in his notebooks. While he composed a number of new poems that would slowly begin to reach the public, Dudley Randall was content to focus on honing his writing skills. He moved from the employ of the Ford Motor plant to that of the U.S. Post Office, married for a second time, and continued to write poetry. World War II would be the shaping experience of Randall's life. In July 1943 he was inducted into the U.S. Army, was trained in the Signal Corps, went overseas in 1944, and served in the South Pacific theater.

After military service Randall returned to Detroit in 1946 and resumed his position in the U.S. Post Office but became a clerk as opposed to the carrier he had been before being drafted. He decided to continue his education. Taking advantage of the benefits of the "G.I. Bill of Rights" extended to those who had served in the military during World War II, he enrolled at Wayne State University. He attended as a full-time student during the day and worked in the post office in the evening. Working in the evening did not prevent him from being active in student affairs at Wayne. He was a staff writer for the *Daily Collegian* and was initiated into Kappa Alpha Psi Fraternity. In 1949, at age thirty-five, he received a B.A. degree in English from Wayne. He began study in librarianship at the University of Michigan and continued to work in the post office. On receiving a master's degree in library science in 1952, he resigned from the post office and accepted an appointment to the library staff at Lincoln University in Jefferson City, Missouri, where he remained until 1954, when he left to join the library staff at Morgan State College (now university) in Baltimore. Randall remained at Morgan for two years, leaving in 1956 to return to Detroit to accept a position in the Wayne County Public Library and, ultimately, to become a catalyst in the Black Arts Movement which emanated from there.

The Wayne County Public Library later became part of the Wayne County Federated Library System, and Dudley Randall advanced in the new entity. He started as assistant librarian and later became the head librarian at the Eloise Hospital Library. Thompson notes that Randall's service as the Eloise Hospital librarian had an impact on his literary interests and quotes him as saying that some of his poems came out of his library experience there. In 1957 Randall married for the third time, this time to a social worker. The Randalls enjoyed a black middle-class lifestyle that the incomes of two black professionals made possible. Moreover, Randall's position allowed him time to expand his work as a poet, and he began to see his work published in little magazines.

Thompson observes that by 1959, at age forty-five, Randall had studied and written poetry for thirty-two years. However, since he had concentrated on writing, not on being published, little of his work that now filled many notebooks in his home had made its way into print. Now, Thompson says,

> All of his prior hard work in developing as a writer, and training in library science, would be harnessed to give birth to the most important publishing company ever created by an African-American to promote the publication, distribution and enjoyment of black poetry—Broadside Press. It was a challenge which Dudley Randall was uniquely qualified to fulfill.

Thompson's emphasis in the first part of this book is on Dudley Randall as a dedicated poet and committed intellectual. The fact that he worked days in a foundry and wrote poetry at night is one manifestation of this. A second manifestation is his earning an undergraduate degree while working full-time. And the fact that he later commuted between Ann Arbor and Detroit in order to engage in full-time graduate study during the day while working full-time in the post office in the evening gives further evidence of his dedication and commitment.

Dudley Randall founded Broadside Press in 1965 as the result of what Thompson characterizes as the initial spark of his decision to publish his well-received poem "Ballad of Birmingham," which he had written as a tribute to the four black girls killed in the September 15, 1963, bombing by the Ku Klux Klan of the Sixteenth Street Baptist Church in Birmingham. He decided to publish it as a broadside, which is a single poem on a single sheet of paper. Other poets allowed him to reprint their work in subsequent broadsides. Thus, Broadside Press was born.

This press was begun with neither blueprint nor savings. It had no financial backing from other writers or investors. It was propelled by Dudley Randall's energy and commitment and funded by money from his librarian's paycheck. His objective was to bring poetry to the people. Thompson's book documents in stellar, scholarly fashion the development of this enterprise. A first-rate scholar, Julius Thompson meticulously records the sources he used, enabling the reader to see, for example, how Hoyt Fuller, the eminent critic, came to the conclusion that Broadside Press had become one of the most important publishing ventures in the history of black literature—and out of the basement of Dudley Randall's home in Detroit. (Dudley Randall died in August 2000, as this was being written.)

By this reviewer's count, some 379 authors and artists were published by Broadside Press. Included among them were Toni

Cade Bambara, Amiri Baraka, Romare Bearden, Lerone Bennett, Jr., Arna Bontemps, Gwendolyn Brooks, Sterling A. Brown, Countee Cullen, Margaret Danner, Ossie Davis, James A. Emmanuel, Hoyt W. Fuller, Addison Gayle, Jr., Langston Hughes, Claude McKay, Haki R. Madhubuti (Don L. Lee), Julian Mayfield, Toni Morrison, and Ishmael Reed.

The foregoing emphases of this book, the first on Dudley Randall the man, the second on the number and caliber of authors and artists that were published by his Broadside Press, are supplemented by a third. The third emphasis of this excellent literary work is on the reciprocal influence of Broadside Press on the Black Arts Movement in Detroit and of the movement on Broadside Press. This book belongs in every library that considers itself to be a resource for students of black literature. Any institution which presumes to offer a program in black studies and which does not include this book in its collection is woefully lacking.

It is not clear where black book publishing houses are headed. Most will probably remain niche publishers accommodating the needs of the African-American marketplace. Jeffrey Gambles, a contributor to *Black Issues Book Review* (BIBR), in an insightful article on the top ten black book publishers, observes that some believe black publishing is dangerously on the brink of extinction.* He notes that some black publishing houses have already closed, victims of unrelenting competition from well-funded white publishers. The latter publishers, he says, have seduced black writers and have beaten black publishers in their own market and are publishing books for the African-American market. However, I believe that the next stage for upwardly mobile neo-autoafroimprints is to transform themselves into mainstream

---

*Jeffrey Gambles, "Trailblazers: Top Ten Black Publishers," *Black Issues Book Review,* September–October 1999, pp. 25–27.

small presses. I do not believe that many of them will make it to this level. Of the ten top black book publishers, I feel that Genesis Press will get there first. My reasons for this belief will become clear further along as I discuss this imprint in some detail.

FOUR PILLARS OF THE AUTOAFROIMPRINT

Du Bois: Pillar of the Autoafroimprint

W. E. B. Du Bois is arguably one of the most eminent black scholars produced in this nation. While not the first African American to earn a Ph.D., he was the first to do so at Harvard University. (Interestingly, the first African American to earn a Ph.D. was Patrick Francis Healey, who was born in 1834, attended Holy Cross, was ordained as a Catholic priest, and taught at Holy Cross. He then went to Belgium and earned a Ph.D. at the University of Louvain there. A year later he became a philosophy professor at Georgetown University in Washington, D.C. He became the first African American to head a primarily white university when Georgetown appointed him as its president. He died in 1910 and is buried on the campus.) Du Bois, after qualifying for a B.A. degree at Harvard in 1890, became a fellow in the Harvard Graduate School. He managed to get a grant from the Slater Fund which made it possible for him to spend the period 1892–1894 studying and traveling in Europe, notably at the University of Berlin. There he studied economics, history, and sociology under such men as Adolf Wagner, Heinrich von Treitschke, and Max Weber. This prepared him well for the role that he was to play as a scholar, author, and teacher when he returned to the United States. After taking his Ph.D. at Harvard be began an academic career.

Du Bois was professor of Greek and Latin at Wilberforce University in Ohio from 1894 to 1896. (While I have no evidence to sustain my hypothesis, I believe that Du Bois may have had some influence on the incipient publishing efforts which manifested themselves in Xenia, Ohio, while he was teaching at Wilberforce University.) Du Bois taught at the University of Pennsylvania from 1896 to 1897. In 1897 Du Bois was recruited by Horace Bumstead, the president of Atlanta University, to supervise the sociology program and to direct a series of conferences on Negroes which Atlanta was sponsoring. In 1910 Du Bois left Atlanta University to edit *The Crisis Magazine.* He returned to Atlanta University in 1934 and remained there until his retirement in 1944.

Du Bois' eminence as a scholar and as the founder of the study of the phenomenon of race and of the black family is uncontested. As one of the leading lights in the fledgling Atlanta University Press in 1898, he is a major star in the autoafroimprint firmament. At the same time, he was being published by a mainstream Chicago publisher. He established the *Phylon* magazine at Atlanta University in 1940. His *Dusk of Dawn* was brought out by Harcourt, Brace and Company in 1940. When the Clark Atlanta University Press was reestablished in 1999, its first book was comprised of articles from *Phylon.* He was truly one of the wind currents under the wings of the phoenix.

In 1998 we commemorated the one-hundred-thirtieth anniversary of the birth of William Edward Burghardt Du Bois and the thirty-fifth of his death. That year, too, we marked the ninety-fifth anniversary of the publication of his seminal work, *The Souls of Black Folk,* and the thirtieth anniversary of its first reprinting by the Johnson Reprint Corporation. This book, which I consider to be one of the most significant black books published in this country, speaks to us today as meaningfully as it did at the beginning of the twentieth century. Tony Monteiro, in the article "W. E. B. Du Bois: Scholar, Scientist, and Activist" (archives, W. E. B. Du Bois Virtual University, members.tripod. com/~DuBois/mont.html), says that this book is a unique Du Boisian effort to philosophically address the problem of race and the failure of American pragmatism to provide a philosophical framework for a social science of race. Monteiro goes on to point out that at Harvard DuBois had studied philosophy under William James and George Santayana. Continuing his philo-sophical studies at the University of Berlin, Du Bois concentrat-ed on the thought of Georg Wilhelm Friedrich Hegel, a German philosopher who was one of the most influential thinkers of the time. I can conclude that Du Bois built the philosophical infra-structure for his phenomenology of race from his study of Hegel's *The Phenomenology of Mind.* In any case, Monteiro goes on to say that *The Souls of Black Folk* can be viewed as a dialogue with Hegel, as well as an inversion of Hegelian idealism. In summing up the significance of *Souls* Monteiro says,

> In the end, *Souls* should be looked upon as a prolegomena of a philosophy of a social science of race. When combined with *The Philadelphia Negro* we have the essential features of a scientific philosophy of race. Moreover, in adapting Hegel's *Phenomenology of Mind* to the specificities of the U.S., and in inverting Hegelian idealism, U.S. social science is equipped with intellectual tools to understand the unique complexities of class and race in the U.S.

Arguably, Du Bois' adaptation of the phenomenology of the mind to the specifics of race in America is not only prolegome-nous, as Monteiro suggests, but entails a central psychic postu-late which was as valid at the end of the century as it was at its start. *The Souls of Black Folk* is not only an enduring testimonial to the rigor of the Du Boisian mind in the analysis of the phenomenon of race but also a matrix for ideas of succeeding generations of thinkers who have written on the subject but who may have come to different conclusions as to the significance of race in the quotidian lives of African Americans. For this memoirist-bibliographer and student of the phenomenon of race, the Du Boisian soliloquy is a paradigm for reflection. Du Bois says,

> The Negro is a sort of seventh son, born with a veil, and gifted with second-sight in this American world,—a world which yields him not true self-consciousness, but only lets him see himself through the revelation of the other world. It is a peculiar sensation, this double-consciousness, this sense of always looking at one's self through the eyes of others of measuring one's soul by the tape of a world that looks on in amused contempt and pity. One ever feels his twoness—an American, a Negro: two souls, two thoughts, two unreconciled strivings: two warring ideals in one dark body, whose dogged strength alone keeps it from being torn asunder.

Surely, the spirit of the black intellectual has been riven by this psychic shearing. The rift can be tracked in the writings of black thinkers from the turn of the twentieth century to this very day. This is not to say that this torment is universally felt among black Americans, because that is not so. There is and has always been a coterie of blacks who do not feel any ambivalence at all as regards the matter of their race.

Some blacks find their "self" easily, without ambiguity and without the sense of double consciousness experienced by others. They seem to manage to absorb, or be absorbed seamlessly by, the culture in which they find themselves, their race notwithstanding. Or put in other terms, by force of will they adapt socially to the society in which they live. This psychic shearing based on the sense of double consciousness is not experienced exclusively by African Americans. Further on, in my explication of a text by Abdourahman Waberi, I will demonstrate that it is felt by blacks in other than American cultures.

As a phenomenologist of race, interested in social adaptability (or integration) as exemplified by the foregoing observation on the adaptability of some blacks to the social context, I was taken by what seems to me to be a clinical parallel which came to my attention. I find this parallel in a response made by a physician to a question from the audience after a panel discussion on ailments of the heart, which I attended recently. The physician, who was white, was asked by a woman, who appeared to be Hispanic, to comment on the phenomenon of ethnically centered ailments. The physician, a board-certified cardiologist, responded categorically. He replied that "culture overwhelms ethnicity." To my mind, and to that of most of the laypeople in that room, he was saying that when persons move from one ethnic culture to another, the new culture dominates any propensity to ethnic-centered ailments. My fond hope is that at some point social scientists will be able to categorically posit such a proposition regarding the preponderance of racial tolerance over racism.

Unlike those blacks who easily adapt to multiethnic settings, there are those who isolate themselves in a black ideological ethnic circle of consciousness that intersects with no other. Still others migrate to circles of ideological ethnic consciousnesses which interact anywhere from marginally to not at all with others. Du Bois anticipated this in *Souls of Black Folk* when he said that some blacks "segregate themselves from the group-life of both white and black, and form an aristocracy, cultured but pessimistic, whose bitter criticism stings while it points out no way of escape."

The symbolic, huddled mass of freedmen which Du Bois observed in 1903 from his intellectual Mount Pisgah has dispersed over the nearly one hundred intervening years. The descendants of those seventh sons of 1903 today pursue disparate visions of the Promised Land. As the light of the dawn of the twenty-first century dispels the shadows of the night of the twentieth, a present-day thinker cannot help but notice that, if it ever was a monolith, the black population of America will not be such in the twenty-first century. There is no principle or concept that can or will ever capture the hearts of all of us. What is ironic in this ideological shift within the black population is that the bitter criticism that stings while it points out no way of escape, and which Du Bois noted as coming from a cultured but pessimistic aristocracy that has segregated itself from black group-life, now comes from the black underclass and is directed at the burgeoning black middle class. The criticism by this alienated cohort of fellow blacks is now the spark that generates the feelings of the twoness of soul, of thought, and of unreconciled strivings that one ever felt at the twilight of the twentieth century. It is the anguished, tortured consciousness of being black and being middle class.

A poignant example of this came to attention some time ago during a PBS *Frontline* program entitled "The Two Nations of Black America," telecast as a Black History Month feature. There we saw the "dream team" Harvard University Black Studies faculty commiserating on the "two nations" that are exemplified today in the black community. Most poignantly we saw Henry Louis Gates, Jr., Du Bois Professor of the Humanities and chairman of the department, in genuine anguish over his privileged position vis-à-vis the "brothers" that he passes every day in the street on his way to his office in Harvard Square. Having been a beleaguered black dean at a white college during the black student uprising in the late 1960s, I was intrigued by Professor Gates's report of his own activism while he was a student at Yale in the 1960s. It was an equally intriguing experience to perceive his obvious anguish in responding to his tortured conscience at being black and comfortable as a tenured professor at Harvard University. As I listened to the comments of Professor Edley of Harvard Law School, I could not help but think of his former colleague Derrick Bell who, as a matter of conscience, could not remain as a professor of law at Harvard, given his perception of Harvard Law School's failure to appoint a reasonable number of blacks to its tenured ranks.

The peculiar sensation of double consciousness endures at century's end. However, the sense of always seeing one's "self" through the eyes of others, of measuring one's soul by the yardstick of a world that looks on, is now experienced from the perspective of fellow blacks who look on more in anger or envy than in amused contempt or pity.

Alain Locke

Another distinguished member of the autoafroimprint brain trust was Alain Locke, the founder of The Associates in Negro Folk Education, a 1921 autoafroimprint. Locke was probably the most distinguished academic of the period after Du Bois. He graduated from Harvard with honors and was the first African-American student to be chosen as a Rhodes Scholar. His 1925 book *The New Negro* made him a nationally known figure. He too, in thirty years on the Howard University faculty, can be said to be one of the machine tools that fine-tuned a legion of scholars. He was the first African-American president of the American Association for Adult Education. His contribution through the publications of Associates in Negro Folk Education is immeasurable.

Carter G. Woodson

The third pillar undergirding the autoafroimprint edifice was Carter Godwin Woodson, a distingushed teacher and scholar in his own right. He earned a doctoral degree from Harvard in 1912, the second black to do so, Du Bois being the first. A teacher and principal in Washington, D.C., Woodson founded The Association for the Study of Negro Life and History in 1915. The following year he began publishing the *Journal of Negro History* for which he wrote hundreds of articles and book reviews. Known as the "Father of Black History," in 1926 Woodson created the Negro History Week observance, which came to be celebrated in February of each year. In 1976, when the nation was celebrating its bicentennial, the observance was extended over the entire month and has been observed since as Black History Month. The books published by The Association for the Study of Negro Life and History, Inc., and its Associated Publishers, Inc., represent a significant contribution to the black history canon. (Charles H. Wesley contributed to the revised edition of Woodson's *The Negro in Our History*, which Associated Publishers brought out in 1990.)

Charles H. Wesley

Charles Harris Wesley, the fourth pillar of the autoafroimprint movement, personally undergirded two of the four publishing enterprises. As I suggested earlier, the seventeen editions of his *History of Alpha Phi Alpha: A Development in College Life*, published by Foundation Publishers from 1935 to 2000, speak to his support of that imprint. Additionally, no fewer than five of his historical works were published between 1955 and 1972 by Associated Publishers, Inc. This imprint has reprinted no fewer than three of Wesley's works since his death in 1987. Dr. Wesley was a contributor to *A Documentary History of the Negro People in the United States 1910–1932*, which was edited by Herbert Aptheker, the distinguished historian and published by the Carol Publishing Group in 1973. Also, Wesley was a consulting editor for the *Afro-American Encyclopedia* published by Educational Book Publishers in 1974.

PUBLISHERS

Mainstream Press Offerings, 1939–1964

Between 1939 and 1964, significant nonfiction books by black authors were brought out by mainstream presses and by three newly emerged black trade publishers. The University of Chicago Press published E. Franklin Frazier's *The Negro Family in the United States* in 1939. In 1940, Harcourt, Brace and Company published W. E. B. Du Bois' *Dusk of Dawn: An Essay toward an Autobiography of a Race Concept.* In 1941, the Macmillan Company published W. C. Handy's autobiography, *Father of the Blues,* which was edited by Arna Bontemps. The year 1943 brought Roi Ottley's *New World A-Coming: Inside Black America* from Houghton Mifflin.

As World War II ended in 1945, St. Clair Drake's *Black Metropolis: A Study of Negro Life in a Northern City* came out under the imprint of Harcourt Brace. In 1947 A. A. Knopf published the first edition of John Hope Franklin's *From Slavery to Freedom: A History of American Negroes.* (McGraw-Hill brought out the eighth edition of this book in 2000.)

The year 1948 saw Arna Bontemps's *The Story of the Negro,* a children's history of blacks beginning in Africa, come into print from A. A. Knopf. This book won the Jane Adams Children's Book Award in 1956.

In 1949 Harper published *Annie Allen,* a book of poetry by Gwendolyn Brooks. This book won the 1950 Pulitzer Prize, the first for an African-American poet.

J. Saunders Redding's *On Being a Negro in America* was published by Bobbs-Merrill in 1951.

I Wonder as I Wander: An Autobiographical Journey, the Langston Hughes memoir, was published in 1956 under the Rinehart imprint.

E. Franklin Frazier's *Black Bourgeoisie* was published in 1957 by Free Press.

Paul Robeson and Lloyd Brown's *Here I Stand: An Autobiography* was published by Othello Associates in 1958. Also in 1958, Martin Luther King, Jr., wrote *Stride toward Freedom* which was published by Harper. This book detailed the Montgomery bus boycott and the philosophy of nonviolent protest.

Black Presses

Robert Fleming, in his fact-filled, well-written, and insightful handbook, makes the observation that with thousands of small presses operating in America today, only a modest twenty of that number are run by African Americans.* He cites the following eleven: Black Classic Press, Arabesque/BET, Genesis Press, Urban Ministries, Inc., Writers & Readers, African American Images, Third World Press, Pines One Publications, Black Words, Africa World Press, and Just Us Books.

I would add another—Johnson Publishing Company, publishers of *Jet* and *Ebony* magazines. I add this autoafroimprint because of its substantial book publishing arm which brought out Lerone Bennett's remarkable *Before the Mayflower: A History of Black America* in 1962. Its backlist includes many excellent nonfiction works.

W. Paul Coates and his Black Classic Press, founded in 1978, merit a special mention here for their contribution to the black nonfiction book canon and to the advancement of black nonfiction authors. The credo of this autoafroimprint says it all: "devoted to publishing obscure and significant works by and about people of African descent." This commitment, in consonance with the on-demand services provided by their affiliate BCP Digital Printing, augurs well for black nonfiction books and their authors in the twenty-first century.

---

*Robert Fleming, *The African American Writer's Handbook: How to Get in Print and Stay in Print*, One World/Ballantine, 2000.

Mainstream Press Afroimprints, 1965–1993

Between 1965 and 1993, ten significant nonfiction books authored by blacks and published by mainstream presses during the era from 1965 through 1993 come to our attention. By year of publication they are:

1965   *Malcolm X: The Autobiography of Malcolm X*, as told to Alex Haley, Grove Press

1965   *Manchild in the Promised Land*, by Claude Brown, Macmillan

1967   *The Crisis of the Negro Intellectual: A Historical Analysis of the Failure of Black Leadership*, by Harold Cruse, Morrow

1967   *Black Power*, by Stokely Carmichael and Charles Hamilton, Random House

1969   *The Militant Black Writer in Africa and the United States*, by Mercer Cook and Stephen Henderson, University of Wisconsin Press

1978   *The Declining Significance of Race: Blacks and Changing American Institutions*, by William Julius Wilson, University of Chicago Press

1984   *When and Where I Enter: The Impact of Black Women on Race and Sex in America*, by Paula Giddings, Morrow/Avon

1990   *The Content of Our Character: A New Vision of Race in America*, by Shelby Steele, St. Martin's Press

1993   *W. E. B. Du Bois: Biography of a Race (1868–1919)*, by David Levering Lewis, Henry Holt & Company (The first volume of this work won the Pulitzer Prize for biography in 1994.)

1993   *Race Matters*, by Cornel West, Beacon Press

These ten books complete the canon of the period that I characterize as the afroimprint surrogacy period. While it is always risky to generalize from a limited sampling taken over a restricted time period, there does seem to be some justification for doing so in this instance. All ten books included are the products of mainstream presses. All ten come from the pens of black authors. Each in its way manifests a certain autocracy in its expression and/or interpretation of the black experience. I suggest that the growing influence of the autoafroimprint and its stable of successful authors was not without influence here. More than had previously been the case, mainstream publishers began to see the wisdom of publishing books by blacks more on their (blacks') terms.

This is not to say that there was general satisfaction with the types of books by and about blacks which the mainstream press was bringing out at the time. Geoffrey Jacques, who has monitored such things in articles in *Publishers Weekly*, had some interesting and relevant observations on the subject in an article in the December 9, 1996, issue.

In annotating several African-American-oriented books which were scheduled for publication in 1997, Jacques observed that they were the types of books formerly published by niche publishers but which now were being brought out by mainstream houses. These were examples, Jacques says, of the pitfalls that await publishers that haphazardly rushed to satisfy the burgeoning black market. Very frankly, the titles do suggest, at the very least, something less than uplifting reads. I would categorize them as demeaning. Jacques quotes Blanche Richardson, a freelance book editor and manager of Marcus Books in Oakland, California, who says of these books:

They're insulting, humiliating, disgusting. . . . Why do they assume this is what we want? Even if an African-American came up with these titles I would strongly recommend they change them.

A subjective view of black nonfiction books and of the black nonfiction book environment awaits you, gentle reader! It is based on what this writer believes is a representative sampling of such books published here between 1995 and 2000.

DUNBAR BLACK BOOK BIBLIOGRAPHY

The Dunbar 500: Black Books, 1995–1997

A look at the types of books that appear in this sampling of the canon of such books published in America is instructive. Using bibliographical data that was available, I classified the books according to content. Twenty-seven of them were arbitrarily categorized as memoirs. Some of these could also be seen as autobiographies. These twenty-seven were authored by Keith Boykin, John Henrik Clarke, Daryl Davis, Tom Dent, Charles W. Dryden, Harry B. Dunbar, Jocelyn Elders, Gary Franks, Sam Fulwood, Grace Halsell, Eddy L. Harris, Grant Hill, bell hooks, Jane Lazarre, James McBride, Kweisi Mfume, Jill Nelson, Tamar Nikurdse, Barack Obama, Colin L. Powell, Ed Tiller, Anthony Walton, Gregory Howard Williams, Lydia F. Williams, Montel Williams, Bruce Wright, and Andrew Young.

Seventy-three of the five hundred books, excluding the twenty-seven classified above as memoirs, can be seen as autobiographies or biographies. Malcolm X is the subject of four of them. Three of them treat Jesse Jackson. There are three focusing on Louis Farrakhan and three on Jackie Robinson. Thelonius Monk, B. B. King, and Denzel Washington are each the subject of two books.

The remaining autobiographies/biographies are about an unnamed working-class black and about Muhammad Ali, Marcus Allen, Louis Armstrong, Arthur Ashe, Benjamin Banneker, Donald Bogle, Arthur M. Brazier, Ron Brown, Willie Brown, Donald Clarke, Johnnie L. Cochran, Jr., Bill Cosby, Sammy Davis, Jr., Frederick Douglass, Charles R. Drew, Jocelyn Elders, Charles Evers, Roswell M. Field, John Fraim, Buck Colbert Franklin, Whoopi Goldberg, Carl R. Green, John Howard Griffin, Frank W. Hale, Jr., Thomas Hauser, Michael A. Hobbs, Ellen Holly, George Moses Horton, Annie M. Hunt, Michael Jackson, Jamaica Kincaid's brother Devon, Jackie Joiner-Kersee, Deacon Jones, Le Roi Jones, Martin Luther King, Jr., Rayford W. Logan, Nat Love, Louis Martin, Shadrach Minkins, Elijah Muhammad, Stuart Nicholson, Shaquille O'Neal, John P. Parker, Paul Robeson, Bayard Rustin, Tupac Shakur, Al Sharpton, Billy Strayhorn, Kathryn Talalay, Clarence Thomas, Sojourner Truth, Gregory Howard Williams, and Tiger Woods.

While there is no sample control group of similar books published in a like period before 1995, with which the 1995–1997 list can be compared, there are observations which I feel can be made *ex cathedra* regarding the one hundred volumes (of the five hundred) which we have classified as memoirs, autobiographies, and biographies.

Each of the subjects of these books was arbitrarily classified into one of twelve categories: activists, athletes, elected officials, intellectuals, military personnel, performers, religious figures, television personalities, historic figures, federal government officials, civil rights leaders, and unknown. The word "arbitrarily" is used because of judgments made in categorizing them. For example, the Reverends Jesse Jackson and Andrew Young and Minister Louis Farrakhan were classified as activists, rather than as clergymen. The notion of what an intellectual is was generously interpreted, and this author has been included among the twenty-two subjects so classified. In the category of performers, Hollywood actors, jazz artists, and the like have been included. Seven persons whose occupations are undetermined were put into the category of "unknown." Jamaica Kincaid's brother Devon is an example of this categorization. In view of the information above, one can say that in the 1995–1997 era, the subjects of black autobiographies and biographies are represented as follows:

Activists	18
Athletes	13
Civil rights leaders	1
Elected officials	2
Federal government officials	3
Historic figures	8
Intellectuals	22
Military personnel	2
Performers	19
Religious leaders	2
Television performers	3
Unknown	7
Total	100

Twenty of the hundred autobiographies and biographies are by or about persons who are not household names. That is to say, the average reader probably never heard of them before the publication of the books in question. (Yours truly is counted under this rubric.) Athletes, performers, and intellectuals dominate in the memoir, autobiography, and biography sweepstakes.

Black Books in 1998: The Dunbar 700

Over the course of the 1998 calendar year I added 248 books to my sampling, and "The Dunbar 500" became "The Dunbar

700." During calendar year 1998, some of these books were reviewed in the online periodical, "Dunbar on Black Books" (www.queenhyte.com/dobb). Many of them were annotated.

For convenience admittedly, I categorized the books in "The Dunbar 700" into five groups as follows: personalities, history, core issues, inspiration/spirituality, and miscellaneous. These groups of convenience subsume twenty-one classes: autobiography, biography, history, memoir, civil rights, children/sons/ daughters, desegregation/integration, finance/business, general, males, military service, politics, race/racism, religion/church, self-help, society/social analysis/culture, travel, women, World War II, inspiration/spirituality/literature, and a historical novel that I included through inadvertence.

Black nonfiction books, as exemplified in my sampling, had another good year in 1998. Those books in the classes autobiography, biography, history, society/social analysis/culture, and memoir account for 148 of the 248 books in my sampling. The remaining hundred books fall under the classes of civil rights, children/sons/daughters, desegregation/integration, finance/ business, general, males, military service, politics, race/racism, religion/church, self-help, travel, women, World War II, and inspiration/spirituality/literature.

PERSONALITIES

In 1998, autobiographies and memoirs by African Americans, and biographies by or about African Americans who were neither athletes nor notorious criminal social deviates, made it into print via major publishing houses in representative numbers. *Toast of the Town: The Life and Times of Sunnie Wilson,* by Sunnie Wilson, with John Cohassey (Wayne State University Press), and *Defending the Spirit: A Black Life in America,* by Randall Robinson (Dutton), are examples. One of the biographies, *Thurgood Marshall: American Revolutionary,* by Juan Williams (Times Books), is the best biography of a black person that this bibliographer read in 1998. Its scholarship stands with the best in the genre. Also in this group is a memoir entitled *The Color of Water: A Black Man's Tribute to His White Mother,* by James McBride (Riverhead Books), which is the only book in the personalities group to make the *New York Times* nonfiction best-seller list.

When one considers the fact that there are sixty-four entries under this rubric, the point is made that publishers believe that there is great interest on the part of black people in reading about both public and private figures in the black community. There is also considerable evidence that black books are crossing over and being read by whites. In any event, it is clear that publishers now believe that there is an audience for books by and about blacks. This has not long been the case.

WORLD WAR II MILITARY EXPERIENCES

One of the categories which, surprisingly, I found to include more entries than expected is that relating to World War II experiences of blacks in the military. In my online newsletter I had lamented the dearth of memoirs by black veterans of World War II in the period commemorating the fiftieth anniversary of the end of that war. I added eight books in this general category to my bibliography in 1998. In July 1998 I reviewed *Lasting Valor,* by Vernon Baker and Ken Olsen (Genesis Press). It can be said that the paucity of such memoirs is being corrected, however gradually. The category of military service (beyond or before World War II) had five entries in 1998.

CORE ISSUES

The interest in the whole matter of the black family both within and outside the black community explains the forty-nine books which I have grouped in the category of society/social analysis/culture. Add to that the thirty-seven books that make up the categories of civil rights, children/sons/daughters, desegregation/integration, males, and women, and we have what I call the eighty-three-book "core issues" bibliography. The core issues bibliography is, in my view, the most significant collection in the black book canon. Taken as an entity, this bibliography is the backbone of nonfiction black book production. It is a manifestation of the subjects, issues, and ideas germane to the black condition that publishers believe appeal to readers in this country. The overwhelming majority of these books were published by mainstream publishers.

INSPIRATION/SPIRITUALITY

Inspiration/spirituality encompasses twelve books. I add to it the group of six books under the class religion/church. I attribute to this eighteen-book rubric considerably more significance than one might expect, given the small number of books involved. One reason for this is that two of the books on this list are the only ones on the Dunbar bibliography to make the *Wall Street Journal* nonfiction best-seller list in 1998. These books, *In the Meantime: Finding Yourself and the Love That You Want* (Simon & Schuster) and *One Day My Soul Just Opened Up: 40 Days and 40 Nights toward Spiritual Strength* (S.S. Fireside), are both by Iyanla Vanzant, a remarkable woman who exemplifies spiritual strength. A second reason why I give considerable significance to this group of books is because of the remarkable influence which inspiration, spirituality, and religion have in the black community. Publishers of books on religion have noted this. Theola S. Labbe reports in *Publishers Weekly* that general publishing houses are now actively acquiring and publishing religion and spirituality books for African-American readers. She cites the diverse readership which the Reverend T. D. Jakes, a black Dallas minister, is garnering for his books, noting that his then current book, *The Lady, Her Lover, and Her Lord,* sold more than 300,000 copies in the first 100 days after it was released in January 1998. Mainstream religious publishing houses have taken notice of what the secular houses have noticed: that there is a market among blacks for books dealing with inspiration and spirituality.

Black Books in 1999

I do not have a good estimate of the number of the approximately 50,000 trade books that were published in the United States in 1999 that were by and about blacks. However, I added 108 such books to the "Dunbar Black Book Bibliography" (DBBB). I believe that the DBBB, numbering 871 books at the end of 1999, constitutes a representative sampling of such books published in this country since 1995. (Readers will understand that when I use the term DBBB, I am speaking of the "Dunbar Black Book Bibliography" and that when I use the term DOBB, I am speaking of my online periodical "Dunbar on Black Books.")

GENERALIZATIONS ON THE 1999 ADDITIONS TO THE DBBB

I organized the 108 books into categories which are admittedly arbitrary but convenient for my purpose here.

The categories and numbers of titles assigned to each are:

A.	Autobiography/biography	15
B.	Education	2
C.	History	29
D.	Memoirs	13
E.	Cultural diversity	8
F.	Politics	3
G.	Reference	1
H.	Regional	2
I.	Religion/spirituality	11

J.	Self Help	5
K.	Sociology	14
L.	Sports	5
	Total	108

It is reasonable to assume that these subjects/categories are accurate indications of the tastes and interests of the readership which the publishers are targeting. In any case, they reflect what the publishers believe this audience wants to read. In 1998 I observed that the audience for black books included not only black people but people of all races. Further, these books are written by persons of all races. As I also pointed out in 1998, the interest in the subject of slavery is high on the part of both writers and readers. There seems to have been no lessening of interest in this subject in 1999. Seven of the books in that year's addition to the DBBB are on the subject of slavery. One of them, *Denmark Vesey: The Buried History of America's Largest Slave Rebellion and the Man Who Led It,* by David Robertson, is said to throw new light on Vesey and the rebellion he led.

The books in categories A and D include historical figures, Frederick Douglass and Mary McLeod Bethune, for example. Also, Malcolm X, Thurgood Marshall, and Martin Luther King are subjects of books in these categories. While the overwhelming majority of the books added to the DBBB in 1999 were first published in that year, there are exceptions. These exceptions include books that were published as long as forty-five years ago but which received recognition in 1999 as being among the best published in the century. For that reason I added them.

I believe the fact that the history category has twenty-nine entries is of substantial significance. Since I believe that all can profit much from the study of black history, the surge that I have noted in publication of such books over the last five years is an omen, if we accept the admonition of George Santayana that the study of history permits us to avoid the mistakes of the past. The titles of some of these books, in and of themselves, suggest the depth of the studies. *Historians and Race: Autobiography and the Writing of History*, edited by Paul A. Cimbala and Robert F. Himmelberg, is an example. The attention that black history is receiving from university presses, such as those at Indiana University, the University of Texas, and the University of North Texas, is encouraging. The fact that a black press was established at Clark Atlanta University and began publishing in 1999 bodes well. The mammoth *Africana: The Encyclopedia of the African and African American Experience*, edited by Kwame Anthony Appiah and Henry Louis Gates, Jr. (the sole reference work on DBBB for 1999), is an eminent work. African-American literary movements are represented by two significant books: *Dudley Randall, Broadside Press, and the Black Arts Movement in Detroit 1960–1995*, by Julius E. Thompson, and *A Renaissance in Harlem: Lost Voices of an American Community*, edited by Lionel C. Bascom. The latter book, a collection of essays produced by Works Progress Administration writers between 1934 and 1939, includes writing by Ralph Ellison and by Dorothy West, both of whom were to become distinguished writers. In the online edition of "Dunbar on Black Books" I gave close attention to Thompson and his work during Black History Month.

The eleven books in category I, religion/spirituality, form a significant block for my purposes here, given the importance of religion and spirituality in current American life. Gustav Niebuhr said that national polls reveal that religiosity runs higher in the United States than in most other economically developed nations. He adds, however, that those polls don't say much about what people actually believe. The rise in alternative religions in this country has led scholars in the American Academy of Religions to form a separate study group within the academy called the New Religious Movements Group. It is interesting to note that the most successful published black writer in the religious/spiritual field today is a New York–born, self-styled Yoruba princess named Iyanla Vanzant. Author of *Yesterday, I Cried: Celebrating the Lessons of Living and Loving,* which I added to the DBBB in 1999, she had three books on the *Wall Street Journal* bestseller list at the same time during that year. Interestingly, the principles of spirituality that she preaches bear more resemblance to Christianity than they do to any Yoruba religion that I know anything about.

Other books in this category are about the black church, and include a so-called exposé of its ministers and congregations; a study by C. Eric Lincoln of contradictions between the American religious ideals of love and brotherhood and the betrayal of those ideals by the white citizens who preached them most; a study of religion in African-American political activism by a University of Rochester professor; and one on sexuality and the black church. In the latter book, the author argues that the "taboo" by the black church against talk about sex has interfered with constructive responses to the AIDS crisis and teenage pregnancies, has fostered intolerance of sexual diversity, has frustrated healthy male-female relationships, and has rendered black and womanist theologians silent on sexual issues. Still another is a "how-to" book written to enable readers to maintain spiritual balance in today's stressful world. Finally, Cornel West, the eminent Harvard professor of religion, grandson of a Baptist minister, "adeptly combined the academic philosopher-theologian with the activist and humanist elements of the African American religious tradition and black nationalist thought," says *Publishers Weekly.*

None of the books in my sampling treat what Niebuhr calls "alternative religions." While there is a rise in the number of adherents to the Muslim faith as represented by the Nation of Islam led by Minister Louis Farrakhan, no book that I am aware of deals with the religion per se. (Several books dealing with Minister Farrakhan have been published in the last five years, but none focusing on the faith.) The story of alternative religion in the black community is yet to be told.

The fourteen books in category K, sociology, cover a wide range of subjects, most dealing with issues impacting the black community. These subjects can be itemized as race relations, AIDS, inner-city life, police relations, desegregation, racism, blacks and gays, and black relationships. They were written by a varied group and constitute an excellent sampling of the bibliography of the 1999 nonfiction black books produced in this country. Their authors include a white radical turned conservative; a white female Yale professor; a journalist and professor of social science at the University of Pennsylvania; a New York University professor of journalism; a noted civil rights lawyer; a white Westchester County, New York, journalist; and an educational sociologist at the University of Oklahoma who is "on a mission to help as many white people as I can to learn more about black Americans," to mention some but not all.

A book by Denene Millner and Nick Chiles, on the differences between male and female perspectives on love among African Americans, is included under this rubric, as is another edited by Eric Brandt on "the volatile relationship which exists between blacks and gays despite their shared experiences of discrimination."

Three other books in this category warrant a comment here, each for its own reason. The first, *Coal to Cream: A Black Man's Journey beyond Color to an Affirmation of Race*, by Eugene Robinson, commends itself to our attention. In this book, Robinson, a foreign correspondent in the South American bureau of the *Washington Post*, compares color, class, and racial identity in the United States with that in South America. (I am reminded of the book *Out of America: A Black Man Confronts Africa*, by Robinson's colleague Keith B. Richburg, who made a similar journey, this to Africa, to find himself as an African American in the spectrum of identity with Africans.) The second book, *Walking on Water: Black American Lives at the Turn of the Twenty-First Century*, by Randall Kenan, compels this mention. In the preface to this book, which is a collection of 200 interviews of young, old, middle-class, and working-class people, the author makes some admissions which *Publishers Weekly* puts into focus. Kenan admits that the book is more of an attempt to answer questions about his own blackness than to figure out what it means to be black in the United States. *Publishers Weekly* observes, however, that Kenan's efforts on this score suffer from an apparent self-absorption born of his fear that he is not black enough. The third book, *We Are Not What We Seem: Black Nationalism and Class Struggle in the American Century*, by Roderick D. Bush, which traces black social movements from the time of Booker T. Washington to the present, looks at the matter from a domestic perspective.

Black Books in 2000

I completed my representative sampling of nonfiction books by and/or about black people published in America since 1995 by adding thirty-four such books, closing out DBBB on 907 such volumes. They are distributed as follows:

A. Autobiography/Biography   5

B. History   4

C. Memoirs   4

D. Sociology   3

E. Sports   3

F. Law   2

G. Religion/Spirituality   2

H. Race	2
I. Cultural diversity	2
J. Education	1
K. Health	1
L. Performing Arts	1
M. Politics	1
N. Psychology	1
O. Reference	1
P. Parenting	1
Total	34

THE NEO-AUTOIMPRINT PHENOMENON

The neo-autoimprint phenomenon is a dimly perceived aspect of the self-publishing trend. I see it as a new microcosm or subculture that has emerged in mainstream book publishing. This microcosm is an outgrowth of a trend in the wider society. Blacks who have been a part of the wider society, even if only marginally, are taking skills that they developed there and applying them, by their own lights, in their own way, to their own enterprises. The widespread use of the personal computer has been and is a catalyst. Applying skills learned in the mainstream, black individuals sit in their dens, home offices, and basements and turn out manuscripts about black people and the issues which impact them. These same individuals direct the development of these manuscripts into books which have all the characteristics of books brought out by mainstream publishing houses. Close study shows that while there are often no outward indications of it, these books can be clearly identified as the work of a single person. That is, the writing of, the contracting for, and the manufacture of the book were all under the direct personal management of, and at the expense of, the author. These authors, as BIBR has said, "are creating an exciting self-publishing industry, one that in many ways is more dynamic and cutting edge than establishment publishing." These books belong to our neo-autoimprint canon.

The case can be made that black periodicals have played significant roles in promoting the afroimprint. As far back as 1910, W. E. B. Du Bois, then the director of publicity and research for the National Association for the Advancement of Colored People (NAACP), presented a proposal for a monthly magazine. This gave rise to *The Crisis Magazine,* now the longest-running black periodical in the nation. In the *New York Times Book Review* (February 28, 1999), Michael Anderson characterized *The Crisis Magazine* as a journal unmatched in its impact on the intellectual life of black America. This periodical has carried reviews of afroimprints and articles by black writers and, historically, has been a supporter of black books and authors. In 1999 Sondra Kathryn Wilson edited a book of stories, poetry, and essays taken from *The Crisis Magazine.*

The Johnson Publishing Company magazines *Jet* and *Ebony* have given publicity to black imprints other than their own. Essence Communications, Inc., publisher of *Essence* magazine, launched Essence Books in 1995 and has published such titles as *Hard Road to Glory,* Arthur Ashe's three-volume history of African Americans in sports. The listing of best-selling black books that *Essence* publishes is the only such listing of which this reviewer is aware.

The *Black Issues Book Review* also warrants our attention as we focus on the support provided to autoafroimprints by black periodicals. This magazine, which comes out six times a year, began publishing in 1999. As a bibliographer of black nonfiction books, I find it to be squarely on the mark. William E. Cox, its president and editor in chief, has commented on the conventional wisdom that black men do not read. He observed that as writers like Guy Johnson, Ellis Cose, Nelson George, Omar Tyree, Walter Mosley, and others produce novels that speak to us, more and more black men are reading fiction. He then went on to signal the intent of BIBR to contend with the old saw that holds that to keep a secret from a black man one needs only to put it in a book and label it nonfiction. He says of BIBR, "Serious, issue-oriented nonfiction remains our genre of choice." This focus is evident throughout every issue of the magazine. Serious nonfiction authors such as Robin D. G. Kelley and Ralph Wiley have been featured in the pages of this magazine.

Regular features of this journal are insightful articles that, taken together, constitute an in-service course for those of us who manage autoafroimprints. The persons conducting these "courses" are a veritable faculty in these publishing classes. There one can find essays by Keith Boykin, Adrienne M. Johnson, Melody M. McDowell, Dr. Rosie Milligan, Victoria Christopher Murray, Gwen Osborne, Asheya Paige, and Ronda Racha Penrice, among others. This magazine is the best professional journal serving the needs of autoafroimprint managers of which I am aware. BIBR maintains a website where many useful articles from the printed magazine have been archived.

Black newspapers such as the *Chicago Defender*, the *Pittsburgh Courier*, and the *New York Amsterdam News* are longtime supporters of afroimprints. On a weekly basis, the latter newspaper, with which I am most familiar, in the last five years has carried reviews of significant black books. Also, it regularly carries news stories about black authors and their books. The regular reviews by Kwame Okoampa-Ahoofe, Jr., are and have been insightful. The news stories and reviews by Cathy Connors and Herb Boyd are timely.

Many of the smaller black newspapers carry reviews and publicity items about black books and their authors if the author, a publicist, or publisher supplies them. My own experience with the *Indianapolis Recorder* and the *Norfolk Journal and Guide* suggests this.

The Internet provides an unmatched resource for author-publishers to find and connect with their audiences at reasonable cost. My Queenhyte imprint and its "Dunbar on Black Books" periodical, located in cyberspace at its own domain (www.queenhyte.com), is an exemplar. As Ishmael Reed observed in the instance I cited earlier, cyberspace gives us the ability to reach audiences unheard of during the sixties. The aim of "Dunbar on Black Books" has been to reach that admittedly small audience of persons interested in serious nonfiction books by black authors. Through my website, I have done so and have developed a following which numbers in the hundreds. The profile of Iyanla Vanzant, the best-selling author specializing in self-help and spirituality, is the most popular essay that I have published on the website. Her webmistress saw it out there in cyberspace and made a link from the Vanzant website to mine. It has been my "best-seller" since June 1998 when first published. Without cyberspace it is unthinkable that I could have tapped Iyanla Vanzant's substantial audience.

Black Book Review Online, located at the QBR.com domain, is the Internet version of the print magazine *The Quarterly Black Review.* It is an excellent periodical promoting black books with aplomb. Its mission statement, presented on the website, says that it was created to "lay claim to the many authors who write for and about us; to give them praise or admonishment; to turn their insights into personal reflection or action. That is why QBR *The Black Book Review* was born." I confess that I have not seen the printed edition of this periodical. Having said that, I take issue with *Black Book Review Online* on its claim to be "the only review dedicated to books about the African-American experience." "Dunbar on Black Books" has been reviewing such books since November 1996.

NEO-AUTOIMPRINT

Emerging in the early 1990s, these imprints founded by "literary entrepreneurs," as the African American Online Writers Guild has dubbed them, are the successors to the 1960–1970 new era autoafroimprints that I spoke of earlier. Self-generated by blacks, the subjects of their books may or may not center on blacks or issues that impact us. Even in instances where they do, it may not be at all evident that the imprint is black-controlled. Genesis Press, which I mentioned earlier in connection with its *Lasting Valor,* by Vernon Baker, is an exemplar of the neo-autoimprint, the 1990s species of the phoenix. At the very least, it is from among them that I believe will emerge the first black-controlled mainstream book publishing company.

BLACK NONFICTION BOOKS: A BIBLIOMEMOIRIST'S PERSPECTIVE

For a memoirist who is also a bibliographer, the urge to blend the two interests is irresistible. A memoirist's focus, let's face it, is on the first part of the word memoir: "me." A bibliographer's focus is, of course, on books. It is clear to my readers that I am a bibliomemoirist, that is, a person who seeks the "me" in books that he reads. As I have said earlier in this book, as a literary narcissist I look in the stream of literature to see my reflection. It goes without saying that as a bibliomemoiric author I readily insinuate myself into the context of the writings of others. Book reviews, critiques, and the like are ready venues.

I did my first book reviews for *Multicultural Review* in 1995. Also in 1995, I began doing a regular online monthly column on books by and about blacks for *American Visions* and have been sharing my opinions on nonfiction books by and about black people every month since, as I compiled the 1995–2000 Dunbar

Black Book Bibliography. I have been fascinated by the discussion and debate that has accompanied the surge in publication of black books.

All of this reminds me of a colloquy between two members of the Afro-American Culture and Arts Forum who were appalled at some aspects of *Push*, by Sapphire, and were discussing it in the context of a June 1996 op-ed piece in the *Wall Street Journal*, by Vaughn A. Carney, a black writer and attorney living in Vermont. In a nutshell, Sapphire is the *nom de plume* of Ramona Lofton, a black woman of about 50 years of age. *Push* is the story of a 16-year-old black girl named Precious, whose father abuses her, rapes her, fathers two children by her.

In his op-ed piece, Vaughn lamented the already-building media hype for *Push*, "the latest celebration of African-American dysfunction." He disdained the "morbid fascination with the most depraved, violent, misogynist, vulgar, low-life element in the African-American experience" which seemed to him to be an engine driving a segment of the publishing industry. My comment, verbatim, from the sidelines follows.

In my opinion, one of the things that we blacks must do is acknowledge that there are those among us who (1) find this acceptable and/or are, at the very least, ready to capitalize on it and (2) believe that like all other ethnic groups, blacks are entitled to engage in whatever folly or self-disparagement they please, without regard to the feelings of those of us whose ethnic pride forces us to temper our portrayals of our people and to consider our actions, utterances, and writings in the context of how they reflect on us as a people.

In this age when, at whatever hour, we turn on our television sets and see shameless people of all stripes, blacks included, engaging in wanton exhibitionism and glorification of their shame, the rest of us must learn to emotionally distance ourselves from the tendency to feel shame rising out of our racial kinship with them. There are two ways that we can deal with these types of situations.

First, if we have the time, the inclination, and the interest, we can "study" these people the way anthropologists study exotic cultures. One need not identify with the subjects which one studies. As a matter of fact, in serious study, identification with the subjects tends to distort objectivity. On the other hand, being black may be helpful to us in gaining an understanding of these people. We must recognize that because of our kinship we have greater potential for becoming authentic experts on the subjects. In serious circles we will be able to speak with authority. The same logic which says that a Jew rather than a Roman Catholic should head the Jewish Studies Program at Queens College in New York suggests that a black anthropologist should be considered a more credible authority on the "depraved, violent, misogynist, vulgar low-life element of African-American experience." Our scholars need to get out front on this. Where are the heirs to the E. Franklin Frazier "home-grown" authority in the studying of us?

Second, if we do not have the time, the inclination, or the interest to make a serious study of these people, we can redouble our efforts to excel in whatever it is that we do, so that we create a record which serious people can consider when making an assessment of the contributions of black people.

In August 1996, along with other authors, including Sapphire, I was scheduled for a signing of my book, at the National Black Arts Festival Book Market in Atlanta. I arrived at the venue after Sapphire had left. I only saw copies of her book that she had signed and left for fans who might arrive after she had left, so I do not know how her signing went. During the evening, two other authors were alongside me at the signing table. One was the author of a children's book, the other of a novel. Most readers would probably recognize the novel and its author if I were to name them and would no doubt find them as repugnant as *Push*.

I have not read the novel, but did thumb through a copy of it there in the book mart, as he did my book. I believe I got the gist of it, though. My sense is that this book does little to enhance the image of blacks in general, or of the black woman in particular. This author told me that his agent was in discussions which may lead to a contract to make the book into a movie. I can tell you that any movie made from this book (which the publisher recommends not be read by minors) would do less than the book does to enhance the image of blacks, and of black women in particular. End of comment from the sidelines.

THE IMPACT OF CYBERSPACE ON FINDING AN AUDIENCE

Ishmael Reed, one of the earliest of the new era autoafroimprint entrepreneurs, made the astute observation that the cyberspace era gives younger writers the ability to reach audiences unreached during the sixties when African-American writers produced broadsides and saddle-stitched chapbooks. Now, he says,

> . . . more voices will be heard and this period, the most prolific in the history of African American literature, will rise to worldwide prominence, no longer having to obey the tastes of the outsiders in power or the dictates of the establishment-manufactured Talented Tenth.

In my view, Reed's observaton could not be more on the mark. I would add that cyberspace gives older writers the same ability to be heard. The Internet is a remarkable scholarly tool which levels the playing field for researchers. It does so for writers as well. No one knows better than this researcher, author, and publisher. In the 1990 to 1994 period I prepared my manuscript of *A Brother Like Me* for publication without the services of a professional typist. Each of the revisions that I made on the recommendation of my editor was keyed in on a personal computer. I put together my own imprint—Queenhyte Publishers—contracted with a major distributor, and brought the book out in 1995. Nearly all the interchanges with the editor and with our contractors were done electronically, by email, file transfer, or fax.

In the period since 1994, I have been able to take further advantage of the remarkable resources which are provided on the Worldwide Web. As a bibliographer I find it possible to put together a bibliography on any subject imaginable using the resources available there. Further, I am able to search digital texts and do substantial and sophisticated research on books and authors right at the keyboard in my home office. An example is illustrative.

My editor called to my attention the expression "gambling-hell" which I was citing in a quotation from Du Bois' *Souls of Black Folk.* (I suspect that my editor thought that the term might have been "gambling hall.") I checked *The Basic Afro-American Reprint Library* edition from which I took the citation. I had gotten it right. The thought occurred to me that the reprint edition may have made an error and that I should check it against another edition. I dreaded the thought of having to take a day to go into New York City to check this out. In addition to the lost time and the cost of twenty or thirty dollars exclusive of parking when one considers gas, tolls, etc., the task was not appealing.

I remembered that there was a digital edition of *Souls* in the Columbia University library or at the Harvard University library. I could not remember the URL for the Columbia University digital library, but had the thought that the Gutenberg project probably had *Souls* in it. I accessed the Gutenberg site. Sure enough, I found the book and downloaded it in its entirety onto a disk. I searched the text and found "gambling-hell" was indeed the way that Du Bois had written the expression. Also, he had used it in another place in the text in exactly the same way. Within an hour, without leaving my study, I was able to download a copy of a book published in 1903 and to check two items of spelling.

I now have a digital copy of the book on a disk. The whole matter took less than an hour and the only the cost was for the phone call. If I were a graduate student today, I would figure out a way to do a doctoral dissertation based on digital texts that I could access in my study at home. I could write my dissertation here too. No need to go to France and forage about in two dusty old libraries. On second thought, I don't think I would have wanted to miss that.

Works by and about W. E. B. Du Bois, incidentally, are enjoying wide availability on the Worldwide Web. One significant such resource is The W. E. B. DuBois Virtual University (members.tripod.com/~DuBois/mont.html). It was developed by Jennifer Wager, a graduate of the Black Studies department at The Ohio State University. Its mission is to serve as a clearinghouse for information on Du Bois and to spur intelligent scholarship and discussion of his life, legacy, and works. This bibliographer, who has a particular interest in Du Bois' thought as a metaphoric source, considers this source to be an excellent one and has arrogated to himself the status of visiting scholar at The W. E. B. Du Bois Virtual University.

A few of the files in this archive which I have found to be particularly useful include:

A biographical essay on Du Bois, by Tony Monteiro

A bibliography of dissertations on Du Bois

A biography of DuBois, by Jennifer Wager

A bibliography of books about Du Bois

A large number of articles about Du Bois

Profiles of several DuBois scholars

CHAPTER 4

A BIBLIOMEMOIRIST
INDULGES HIMSELF

While I began to read nonfiction books by and about black people in the 1970s at the time of the student unrest, I became a serious devotee of the genre in about 1993. As a volunteer assistant I
became involved with the American Black Book Writers Association, Inc., a Calfornia nonprofit organization which was compiling a database of titles of books by black authors. My interest
in black nonfiction books took off. Since 1994 I have been a full-
time student of the subject. In the course of this study I began
compiling a bibliography which was to be a representative sampling of these books. By the end of 1999 the bibliography included more than 840 titles. These books were coming from a diverse
group of publishing entities. A cursory look at this development
was enough to convince this observer that a phenomenon was
unfolding.

NEO-AUTOIMPRINTS

Genesis Press and Wilbur Colom

Genesis Press, founded by Wilbur Colom in 1993, is a meritorious imprint. This family-owned publishing enterprise is based in Columbus, Mississippi, and operated by Colom who is a lawyer and his wife who is a judge. The notion of founding a publishing company was his wife's, Colom told an interviewer. He had represented clients in the literary field and is a writer whose articles have appeared in major publications. It is therefore not surprising that Genesis Press is an excellent imprint. On the basis of *Lasting Valor*, by Vernon Baker, a nonfiction book published by Genesis Press in 1997, I can say unequivocally that this imprint is already in league with the best of them. A collaborative effort which Genesis is reportedly developing with One World/Ballantine Books promises to move Genesis squarely into the mainstream. In any event, *Lasting Valor* is a must read. I read and reviewed it before I knew anything at all about Genesis Press, or about any of the other books published by it, or about Wilbur Colom for that matter. Genesis Press made the cut for inclusion as an autoafroimprint only after I stumbled upon its website, saw its home page—and the pictures of its principals.

While Genesis Press has in my view already leapt into the mainstream of American book publishing, I believe it to be the most outstanding example of a neo-autoimprint and, since 1990, the only imprint founded by a black which has made it to the mainstream. Founded to publish romance books, it heralds its premier romance imprint as the best in contemporary African-American romance. Genesis publishes Latin romance novels under another imprint. It also puts out general fiction books. It is, I believe, an eminent publisher of nonfiction books.

It is said that first impressions are lasting. For this reviewer, the first impression of Genesis Press was gained from the reading and analysis of its *Lasting Valor*. Simply put, as I have implied in an earlier comment, I was totally convinced that this book had come from a mainstream press. Everything about it was first class. The writing, the editing, the manufacture, and the look and feel of the book contributed to this perception. The fact that Ken Olsen collaborated with Vernon Baker, the author of the book, also lent credence. The fact that *Lasting Valor* is in the company of two other quite mainstream Genesis titles added to the impression. These titles are *Hitler, the War and the Pope*, by Professor Ron Rychlak, and *The Smoking Life: What Do You Think Was in Those Peace Pipes?* by Ilene Barth (1997). To paraphrase W. Paul Coates, a book under the imprint of Genesis Press, whether about the pope or about tobacco, is a neo-autoimprint.

Denise Pines and Pines One Publications

I am indebted to Amy Alexander for showcasing another neo-autoimprint which is clearly in the league with Genesis Press. In a BIBR profile of Denise Pines and her Pines One Publications, I learned of another "class act" in the publishing industry. Denise Pines is a black woman with corporate experience at AT&T. After taking a publishing course at Stanford University in the mid-1990s, she used her seventeen years of experience in marketing and public relations gained from her corporate days and organized her company. In 1997 she left her high-paying salaried position to start her own publishing company in Los Angeles.

As Alexander puts it, Pines knows that she is a lone voice in the publishing community, a black woman publisher who wants to offer readers a fresh perspective on the complexities of black life. Two of the books that she has already brought out are indicators of the level at which Pines One will operate.

The first, *Wall Street Main Street and the Side Street: A Mad Economist Takes a Stroll*, by Julianne Malveaux, foreword by Maya

Angelou, is illustrative. Malveaux is an economist, a writer, and syndicated columnist who has been described as one of the most provocative, progressive, and iconoclastic public intellectuals in the country. She has been on the faculty of the University of California, at Berkeley, and an affiliated scholar at Stanford. She specializes in the study of the labor market and public policy and the impact of such policy on women and people of color. She has also taught economics and African-American studies. This book will be a distinct credit to the Pines One imprint.

The second book, *On Air: The Best of Tavis Smiley: Thoughts on the Tom Joyner Morning Show,* is very likely to resonate in the minds of black readers and to reflect positively on the Pines One bottom line. Tavis Smiley is the well-known host of Black Entertainment Television's *BET Tonight with Tavis Smiley.* This live, call-in show covers current events, celebrities, politicians, and hot-button issues pertaining to African Americans. Reportedly, he earns more than $1 million a year. In 1994 *Time* magazine selected him as one of America's most promising young leaders under forty. He is considered an important voice among black Americans. As this manuscript was being edited, the announcement was made by Black Entertainment Television that Tavis Smiley was being dismissed. I do not know what is behind it all, but I am sure that this book will certainly be given a boost by the dismissal.

Tony Rose and Amber Books

There are other neo-autoimprints which have not reached the level of Genesis or Pines One but which are worthy of attention. One is Amber Books of Phoenix, Arizona. This young enterprise was founded by Tony Rose in 1998. Rose had spent fifteen years in the music industry as a record producer and record company owner before establishing the Amber imprint. It specializes in self-help and career guidebooks for African Americans and has enjoyed rapid success. One of the nonfiction books that it has brought out is *How to Play the Sports Recruiting Game and Get an Athletic Scholarship: The Handbook and Guide to Success for the African-American High School Student*, by Rodney J. McKissic. In 1999 Rose was presented with the Publisher of the Year Award at the second Annual Black History Month Book Fair and Conference in Chicago. Amber Books publications are distributed by three leading book distributors: Ingram, Baker and Taylor, and Koens. Rose was featured in the "Self Publishing" column in the November–December 1999 issue of BIBR. We will be hearing more from this neo-autoimprint. It is a comer.

Harry B. Dunbar and Queenhyte Publishers

Finally, on the subject of the neo-imprint may I be excused for calling attention to my own Queenhyte Publishers. It manages its own proprietary imprint which published *A Brother Like Me: A Memoir*. It operates my website Queenhyte.com which publishes my monthly online newsletter "Dunbar on Black Books." It packages content for a nonprofit imprint. I see it as a modest year-2000 imprint on the Dudley Randall *Broadside Press* model. Its mission is first to publish my own writings and second to promote nonfiction books by and about blacks. I have arrogated to the imprint the role of model/consultant to individuals who have a passion to publish a nonfiction work.

"DUNBAR ON BLACK BOOKS"
ON THE INTERNET

In 1996 I began my online newsletter "Dunbar on Black Books," in which I featured nonfiction books that were published since 1995 by and about blacks. This monthly newsletter was distributed in the Books and Writers section of the Afro-American Culture and Arts Forum, sponsored on the CompuServe Information Service by *American Visions,* the official magazine of the African American Museums Association. In November 1997, after the forum was discontinued, I moved "Dunbar on Black Books" to the Internet. At the invitation of Chet Gottfried, the book designer for my Queenhyte Publishers imprint, I began sharing his domain. In June 2000 I moved "Dunbar on Black Books" to Queenhyte.com, my own domain, where Chet is the webmaster. The newsletter has been online, either at the Afro-American Culture and Arts Forum or in cyberspace, with a new issue every month, without interruption since July 1996.

This puts me among the first to have a serious and stable series online. The experience of commenting on nonfiction books by and about black people in my own venue has been an exhilarating one. Most of the essays in this column are reviews, commentaries, or explications of texts, always on a subject that interests me. I have selected some of the well-received columns for inclusion in this book. Readers who have Internet access are invited to visit the site at www.queenhyte.com/dobb.

OUT OF AMERICA
BY KEITH B. RICHBURG

In April 1997 I wrote a commentary on Keith B. Richburg's controversial book *Out of America: A Black Man Confronts Africa* (Harcourt Trade Publishers, 1998). I said that this book may prove to be seminal as regards the way some African Americans deal with their African ancestry and heritage. I hypothesized that the romanticism with which many now deal with the subject will change. The romanticism will give way. Perhaps more African-American writers will come to deal with the irrelevance of our African ancestry in confronting the problems we face in trying to succeed in the American environment. So what if I can trace my family line to African royalty? Or even to that of current despots whose treacheries are detailed by Richburg? Three years in Africa, where, as a bureau chief for the *Washington Post,* he covered events in Somalia, Zaire, Nigeria, and Cameroon, among other places, brought Richburg to characterize Somalia as the prism through which to view the rest of Africa and, ultimately, as the metaphor for his disillusionment.

Richburg, after viewing the countless ongoing civil wars and tribal clashes during his three-year tour in Africa, while identifying with the innocent victims, came to the realization that:

> . . . even though I looked like them, and might have at some point been mistaken for one of them, I was not like them. I was always on the outside looking in, like a stranger who had wandered aimlessly onto a movie set and ended up in the middle of the film.

Richburg says that traveling around Africa taught him that the tribe continues as the defining feature of almost every African society and that old tribal mistrusts and stereotypes linger, maintaining the potential for violence at any time. He observed this even in the more sophisticated or developed countries like Kenya.

The parade of brutal tyrants who dominate Nigeria, Zaire, Rwanda, Somalia, Liberia, and other countries on the African continent led Richburg to renounce his African heritage and to affirm that he is an American, not an African American. He is troubled by the fact that African-American political personalities and others who come to Africa fawn over these petty tyrants, never seeming to criticize them and continually making excuses for them.

Despite the heat that he appears to be taking for it, Richburg's frank critique of the blind, knee-jerk, romanticized approach of some black Americans to their African heritage may

encourage other writers to speak more openly on the subject of
the irrelevance of our African heritage to the solution of some of
our problems in the black communities of America. What does
our African heritage have to do with our unwillingness or inabil-
ity as a people to censure our leaders who are racist, dishonest,
criminal, or worse? Keith B. Richburg's book may be the tip of
an iceberg.

Subsequent to writing the foregoing, I came upon a review of
this book by William Finnegan in the New York Times Book Review
of March 30, 1997. I felt compelled to respond as follows.

William Finnegan laments the fact that Keith Richburg's
memoir "retains almost nothing of the careful, fact-chasing spirit of his daily reporting." Pray tell, how should Richburg have
infused a fact-chasing spirit into his recounting of impressions
which he gained from the experience of observing wanton and
widespread murder, thievery, despotism, and barbarism for some
three years in several different countries in Africa? Should he
simply have copied from his notebooks the dates, places, and
times when he saw these things? Should he have gotten observations from two independent witnesses in each instance?

Finnegan observes the "unsubtle" take on Africa which
Richburg manifests in this book. He notes that Richburg's prose
"lacks the weight to carry major themes." Finnegan opines that
Richburg's claims to be revealing unpopular truths about the dire
state of Africa ring hollow "in an era when writing off Africa . . .
has long been a popular exercise in the more truculent journals
and think tanks of the developed world." Further, Finnegan
bemoans what he terms Richburg's seeming lack of awareness
that he (Richburg) is making his harsh critique in comfortable
tenured company. But Finnegan's comment that Richburg's
book is one that "remains in the preferred mode of American
publishing today, relentlessly focused on the author's thoughts
and feelings," makes the point that should have been Finnegan's
focus at the start of his review. This book is an exposition of

Keith B. Richburg's impressions drawn from his experiences as a black American in Africa. It is not a subtle presentation of surface observations. It is not necessarily directed at the audiences which have been addressed by the more truculent journals and think tanks of the developed world. I take issue with Mr. Finnegan's argument that Keith Richburg "has poorly served both his American readers and his subject." Mr. Richburg has served at least one member of his American audience well. His frank critique of the lockstep march of many black Americans to the cadence call of afrocentric drillmasters in respect to their African heritage is certain to make some of us think again about our position on this. Finally, I don't know from what planet Finnegan makes his observation that Richburg "seems conveniently unaware that he is in comfortable, tenured company" in saying the things that he says in this book. On this planet, without knowing any more about Mr. Richburg's situation than what I read in the papers, I can tell Mr. Finnegan that Keith Richburg's tenure-protected position with the *Washington Post* may be a financial comfort, but his expressed views on his African heritage probably provide little comfort to him in the African diaspora in America. As a result of my response to William Finnegan's review, I was interviewed on *Adam's World*, a radio call-in show in south Florida.

SPOTLIGHTS

I have featured a number of other writers in DOBB over the years. Several are of special and unique interest. One of them is Iyanla Vanzant.

Spotlight on Iyanla Vanzant

In June 1998 I posted the following profile of Iyanla Vanzant on the "Dunbar on Black Books" website. It has received more "hits" every week than the other thirty-three essays I have published since then.

Iyanla Vanzant is a prolific writer whose work has created a substantial blip on the radar screen of the publishing industry. She is the author of several books which target African-American men and women, books which, as *Publishers Weekly* points out, have proved that they can reach a wider audience. One of them, *In the Meantime: Finding Yourself and the Love You Want*, is on the national charts. A second, *One Day My Soul Just Opened Up*, is reportedly right below the top fifteen. There are 250,000 copies of the first book in print. There are about 235,000 copies of the second. Vanzant's most successful book, *Acts of Faith*, published in 1993, has more than 700,000 copies in print. Two of her other books, *The Value in the Valley: A Black Woman's Guide through Life's Dilemmas* and *Faith in the Valley: Lessons for Women on the Journey to Peace*, have a combined total of nearly a million copies in print in paperback and in hardcover. Who is Iyanla Vanzant? How has she managed this remarkable achievement?

My initial sense of who Iyanla Vanzant is, gained from scanning lists of books and authors to make selections for inclusion in the "Dunbar on Black Books" bibliography, was not unlike that of the disc jockey who said that when he first heard the name Brooke Benton, he thought of an account executive. The manner in which the disc jockey said this clearly implied that before he learned better, he thought that Brooke Benton was a white man. So it is that when I first saw the name Iyanla Vanzant listed as the author of *Acts of Faith*, I made the snap judgment that this was a white woman of middle European descent. Until I learned more than a year later that Iyanla in Yoruba means "great mother," I had no idea of Ms. Vanzant's ethnicity. (This made no difference as regards the inclusion of the book in the bibliography since any book which is about or targets black persons can be included, irrespective of the ethnicity of the author.)

From a 1996 interview by Diane Weathers of *Essence* magazine, I began to get an insight into who this Brooklyn-born Yoruba princess is. First I learned that she is a spiritual counselor, author, and lecturer who has come to her calling by an unusual route. She had a classically troubled childhood marked by all the trauma-producing experiences imaginable. The death of her mother when she was two years of age, her rape by a family member when she was nine, eleven years on welfare, a broken jaw at the hands of an abusive husband, and two nervous breakdowns all suggest that over the forty-two years that she had lived by 1996, the time of the interview, Iyanla Vanzant had acquired considerable firsthand experience with dysfunctional living. What is also clear is that Iyanla Vanzant took the lemons given to her by life and made lemonade. She has become a spiritual counselor *par excellence*. How she did it is inspiring.

Vanzant enrolled at Medgar Evers College of the City University of New York in 1978 and thus took the first step toward getting off welfare. She graduated summa cum laude in 1983. After that she attended the CUNY law school at Queens College, where she earned a Juris Doctor degree in 1988 and passed the bar the same year. Reportedly, she is nearing the completion of a Ph.D. in religious studies at Temple University. She moved to Philadelphia and joined a law firm there as a criminal-defense lawyer. After three years she resigned, providing the following rationale for leaving the firm in 1990:

> I wasn't doing what I was supposed to be doing. I knew if I remained I would become part of the system, and I knew that system was wrong.

It was at this moment that Vanzant had one of the visions that seem to characterize her life. She tells of walking into her office at the law firm and experiencing the room as being without any light at all. She says that she told this to her secretary, who was incredulous, and insisted that the lights were working and suggested to Vanzant that she needed to have her vision checked. Vanzant says of that experience:

> From down deep in my soul the message came to me: You're standing in darkness. So I just walked out. I never told them I quit, I just left.

It is at this point that Ms. Vanzant appears to have responded to a long-felt call to give herself over to Yoruban culture as a way of dealing with life. Just as the biblical Saul of Tarsus had experienced a blinding light on the road to Damascus preceding his conversion, so Iyanla Vanzant experienced total darkness in the office of a Philadelphia law firm before seeing the light of Yoruban culture as an alternative lifestyle and committing herself fully to counseling others in her new faith.

Vanzant's *modus operandi,* as gleaned from the Diane Weathers interview, suggests a priestess with five disciples. Vanzant tells the interviewer that these five, whom she calls her "buds," work, play, and pray full-time out of her home in Maryland. The home is the nerve center of the Vanzant company, "Inner Visions Spiritual Life Maintenance." In the basement office, the business side of the ministry is carried on. It is there that the telephone work, the scheduling of the lectures, and direct sales of her books and tapes are handled. There, too, the efforts and energies of the ancillary functionaries who are part of Vanzant's entourage are engaged: hands-on healers, energy masters, and prayer warriors.

Her home is also organized to advance the spiritual side of the participants. According to Diane Weathers, one doesn't realize that this is the abode of a Yoruba priestess until one goes upstairs. There, yellow notes on door and mirror frames in Vanzant's bedroom, office, and bathrooms are reminders to stay the course: "I will judge nothing that occurs"; "The struggle is over"; "I am a divine daughter"; and "What you see you become."

There are three altars on the premises. At a bedroom altar Vanzant does a daily meditation at 5:30 A.M. On the altar is an amethyst crystal and ashes from the altar of the Dalai Lama. Also found here are images of Ms. Vanzant's spiritual muses: Baba Muktananda, Babaji, Gurumayi Chidvilasananda, Vishnu, and Buddha.

On an altar in her book-lined office sit seven glasses of water and an image of the Black Madonna. It is at this altar that Ms. Vanzant consecrates her eyes, head, mouth, and ears before sitting down at her computer to write.

Once a week, Vanzant visits a third ancestral altar in a room in the basement. Displayed on it are old family photos and pictures of twenty-one legendary African-American women, including Harriet Tubman, Audre Lorde, Queen Mother Moore, and Ida B. Wells. Vanzant explains to a visitor, "I'm standing on my ancestors. They are powerful people who have done so much of the work."

The study of other articles and essays about Iyanla Vanzant and her ministry contributed to my sense of who she is. A 1995 essay by Barbara Campbell, describing the effect that Vanzant had on a large crowd at London's Electric Cinema, is illustrative of the way that Vanzant has built her following and her readership. The thought occurred to me that at about the time that I was classifying her as a middle European white woman, she was a black Yoruba priestess presenting before audiences in England which, as Campbell says, "have a propensity to lap up anything to do with the spiritual and the mystical, all in search of that intangible something they believe exists."

A clear image of Iyanla Vanzant emerged in my mind in the spring of 1998. She is a bright, highly spiritual, well-educated, self-ordained African-American Yoruba priestess. She preaches a powerful message of self-empowerment that meets a need both here and abroad. She is constantly on the road evangelizing and concurrently promoting her writings. Unlike most other "evangelists," she appeals as much to the intellect of her hearers as she does to their emotions. The proof is found in the fact that they buy her books and, evidently, read them.

Spotlight on Abdourahman A. Waberi

African Frenchman, African-American Torment

Another black writer of special and unique interest is Abdourahman A. Waberi. As late as August 22, 1998, he was the most unlikely candidate for inclusion in the roster of writers featured in DOBB. The reason for this was that I had never heard of him or of his writings. Further, if I had run across his name in my scanning of publication lists in search of names of authors of books by and about blacks, the orthography of his name would not have triggered my instinct to pursue it further as a prospect. The name Abdourahman A. Waberi affected me more or less in the same way that the name of Iyanla Vanzant once had. In this instance, my snap judgment was that Mr. Waberi was some Arab who bore no relevance to black books. Happenstance was to teach me otherwise.

During the 1959–1960 academic year I had been a researcher in Paris preparing a doctoral dissertation on selected French men of letters. For some thirty-eight years since 1960, I had planned to return to the City of Light. In August 1998 I did so on a sentimental one-week visit. Chance had it that I picked up a copy of *Le Monde* which contained an article whose title translates into English as "The Blues of Moussa the African." This op-ed essay commends Abdourahman A. Waberi as an eminent member of the roster of authors I cite in DOBB. I knew nothing about him other than what was in this article and that he writes in French. But, to use one of Mr. Waberi's favorite expressions, "Let's move forward."

From the editor's notes which accompanied "The Blues of Moussa the African," I learned that Abdourahman A. Waberi was born in the former French Somaliland in 1965, and since 1985 has lived in France, where he is a high school teacher in a Paris suburb. He is the published author of three nonfiction books about his native country and the conflicts in the horn of Africa. They are *Le Pays sans ombre, Cahier nomade,* and *Balbala,* all three of which were published by the *Serpent à plumes* publishing house. I also learned from this source that in 1996 Waberi was the recipient of the literary grand prize of North Africa. This is the total factual information which I had about him, and that from reading the editor's notes before reading the essay itself. But "let's move forward."

The tradition-honored French scholarly exercise known as the *explication de texte,* in which I had been trained more than forty years ago, came instinctively into play. This technique allows one to draw substantial conclusions about an author based on rigorous analysis of the text of his or her writings. A careful parsing of the text is *de rigueur,* as is a careful factoring in of biographical and other information about the author. Absent these two ingredients, there is great risk of drawing incorrect conclusions.

The considerable internal evidence in Waberi's essay permits a number of conclusions about its author. Even if the photo of him which is part of the presentation had not been there, I would have been able to conclude that the intellectual who wrote this essay is black. A careful parsing of the text led me to conclude that Abdourahman A. Waberi is an authentic French model of the end-of-the-century black, tortured by a Gallic sense of the twoness which being a black African and at the same time a citizen and resident of France arouses in him. I think, despite the linguistic veil which dims the clarity of my intellectual vision, that through the prism of racial kinship I can feel the torment which had scarred Waberi's soul. Without question, this torment is the same as that which in 1903 William Edward Burghardt Du Bois said, in his *Souls of Black Folk*, afflicted American blacks at the dawn of the last century. I speak of the torment that had scarred Waberi's soul because I believe that there is evidence in the text that he had come to terms with it.

My grasp of the French language after an absence of more than thirty-eight years permits little more than a surface understanding of texts that I read *à livre ouvert* in that language. That is, without carefully researching words that could be symbolic or used in an other-than-literal sense, I am not sure that I have seized a possibly subliminal meaning intended by an author. How then do I, after a thirty-eight-year absence from the reading of French texts, or of even visiting the premier French-speaking nation of the earth, have the temerity to do an analysis of a French text in the very capital of French letters? My current presumptuous act can only be explained as an obverse of the temerity which I manifested in 1959 when I did an analysis of the writings of seven white French men of letters to trace the impact on their intellect of certain philosophical currents.

The venue for this cerebral soliloquy on the part of Abdourahman Waberi is the opening ceremony of the World Cup on June 9, 1998, at the Place de la Concorde in Paris. Four players symbolizing different racial/ethnic groups are featured at this event to incarnate the sports comradeship of the thirty-two nations and the four continents convened for this event. One of these symbols, Moussa the African, whose Moslem given name, Waberi tells us, has the purpose in the minds of the conceivers of this event, of uniting all of the Africas, the South and the North, the Mali and the Malawi, black Africa and the Maghreb, the country of the Bafanas and Tunisia. What is clear to me is that the concept resonates in the very being of Abdourahman A.

Waberi. As he sees it, Moussa the African, conceived in the heart of Paris on Tuesday, June 9, 1998, will be easily recognized by every citizen in every quarter of the city.

Waberi begins his essay by soliloquizing on his own first conception of France and Frenchmen, gained as a boy in Djibouti as he observed French military men and members of the French Foreign Legion as they served in his country. They were athletic types with skins bronzed by the African sun. France was, to his adolescent eyes, he says, powerful, crackling with ease and health, devoted to sports and to leisure, unrelated to the intellectualized France he later came to know.

Advancing, Waberi comes to the lack of rapport between France and the immigrants from its former black colonies. He cites the slow-to-heal wounds, and the illusions lost on the other side of the Mediterranean, that frontier before the police barriers and the customs harassments which are faced immediately at the Charles de Gaulle or Orly Airport by those other-than-white-skinned people arriving in Paris from the former black colonies of France. It is here that Waberi demonstrates his understanding of, and kinship with, the sense of the twoness which is felt by those African Americans who are tortured by the reality of being at the same time black and citizens/residents of a nation that does not understand them. France, he says, has business with the great-grandchildren of those who had come to study in the metropolis at the beginning of the century, those who had rubbed shoulders with the French elite of the time. We are far from the period of the black dancers of the Rue Blomet, the belts of bananas worn by Josephine Baker. In the 1930s, he says, Josephine Baker sang, "I have two loves, my country and Paris, always equal, my heart is delighted." Today, he says, Doc Gyneco, the young rapper of West Indian descent, says, "My father was born over there, my mother was born over there. As for me, I was born here." (Gyneco was born in the Clichy section of Paris, of parents from the Antilles.)

Waberi notes that a long, half-century-old river flows between the two refrains and recounts some tumultuous events which seem to explain the transition from the "fusion" of which Baker sang to the separation about which Gyneco raps.

Paris was, Waberi reminds us, a peaceful harbor, an oasis without segregation or discrimination against Afro-American artists after World War II. Numerous were those who chose to be domiciled here, for a season or for life. They included Richard Wright, Duke Ellington, James Baldwin, Chester Himes, Langston Hughes, Claude MacKay, and Deedee Bridgewater, he continues. Then, in a peroration in which, frankly, many of the subtleties escape me, one thing leaps out. There is in France an anti-African bias created by newspapers, through "prosthetic treatises." Blacks in France are stereotyped along the lines of their countries of origin, Waberi argues, enumerating at least twenty-four of these "value judgments without scientific basis," as he calls them.

Waberi's soliloquy led me to conclude that he saw in the "birth" of Moussa the African in the heart of Paris a symbolic promise of a purging of this anti-African bias in the hearts of Frenchmen. This kind of birth, he says, is not given to just any-one.

Spotlight on Gayle Pemberton

Another writer of special and unique interest is Gayle Pember-ton. As a former academic and serious student of black biogra-phy I found great interest in Gayle Pemberton's *The Hottest Water in Chicago: On Family, Race, Time and American Culture* (1992). At the time that I reviewed this book for *Multicultural Review* in 1994, Ms. Pemberton was associate director of Afro-American Studies at Princeton University. She has a B.A. degree in English from the University of Michigan and a Ph.D. in English and American literature from Harvard University. Before joining the faculty at Princeton, she had substantial teaching experience in top-ranked colleges and universities. It is my judgment that she writes well and that *Hottest Water* is worthy of the attention of students of black biography.

Gayle Pemberton and *Hottest Water* have a particular pertinence for me in the study of my generation. Internal analysis of *Hottest Water* suggests that Ms. Pemberton is as close to the age cohort of my daughter as I am to that of her late father. I see my daughter's outlook mirrored in some of the views expressed by Gayle Pemberton. Moreover, I identify with Pemberton's father through the surrogacy of her portrayals of him. Perhaps, too, I am moved by the fact that Pemberton had encouraged her father to write his memoirs and that the two had a secret pact that she would help him write them, but by the time he died on November 12, 1977, he had written only a short passage which she found on three sheets of yellow legal paper.

The thought does not escape me that in my search for data to develop the biography of my age cohort, I may be reduced to sketching it from, among other things, the observations of a person of my daughter's generation. Given this prospect, it is an interesting aside to contemplate the take which she would have on some perspectives which I hold. One example is Pemberton's view of her father's position on fraternities and his devotion to Omega Psi Phi Fraternity in particular. She hates fraternities and finds them useful "only in asserting unpleasant realities, like banal group-think, one-upmanship based upon the acquisition of material goods, backbiting, and other forms of social regression." I wonder if any of this is mirrored in my daughter's view of my devotion to Alpha Phi Alpha Fraternity over fifty-two years. After all, like Pemberton, my daughter had the experience of foreign travel as a high school student and attendance at a highly competitive college, a career in a white-dominated workplace, and limited experience with life in a black-dominated social environment. Alpha Phi Alpha might come off as badly in her estimation as Omega Psi Phi does in that of Pemberton. I suspect, though, that as Pemberton enjoyed the Omega picnics and parties, my daughter enjoyed the Alpha youngsters that she met and socialized with at conventions across this country to which we dragged her over the years.

As a person who sees the early W. E. B. Du Bois as a "retro-model" of his own intellectual life, it is a great source of wonderment to me that Pemberton, a student of Du Bois' work, does not see in the context of Du Bois' migration to "the region of blue skies and wandering shadows" her own and her friends' enjoyment at seeing themselves forming a club called "Les Elus." I wonder too why it is that they did not name their club "Les Elues," given the probability that the members were all women.

Gayle Pemberton's *The Hottest Water in Chicago: On Family, Race, Time and American Culture* is an important book. Pemberton husbands meager documentation she happened upon and creates a masterful sketch of her grandfather, a remarkable man. Her analysis of the notes penciled by him in the margin of his autographed copy of Du Bois' *The Souls of Black Folk* is incisive and her extrapolations are on the mark. The sketches of persons found in this book are well done. The book is a useful, albeit small contribution to black biography. I will reread it many times as I plumb it for more of her perspectives on the life of Lounneer Pemberton, her father. After all, I identify with him.

Spotlight On Vernon J. Baker

Vernon Baker is another writer deserving of attention. His book, *Lasting Valor*, written with Ken Olsen (Genesis Press), is an outstanding book. General Colin Powell noted that it was one of the first full-length biographies of a black World War II infantryman. It fills a gap in the history of World War II that this review-er had decided would never be filled. I have, in my essays in "Dunbar on Black Books" and elsewhere, lamented the dearth of recollections by black World War II veterans coming into print during the period celebrating the fiftieth anniversary of the end of that war. Mindful of the present age of the men who partici-pated in World War II, I had in fact given up any hope that this gap would ever be filled. As Steven E. Ambrose, the historian and author of *Citizen Soldier: The U.S. Army from the Normandy Beaches to the Bulge to the Surrender of Germany*, has said, "Those GIs born between 1924 and 1927 saved Western civilization" ("What We Owe Them," *Wall Street Journal*, May 22, 1998).

It has long been my view that the contribution of the cohort of black GIs born between 1924 and 1927 has not heretofore been clearly articulated by any of its own members. Enter Vernon J. Baker, an African American from Cheyenne, Wyoming, who fought the racism manifested by his white commanding officers as well as that of the fascists and Nazis in the Italian campaign in 1944 and 1945. This book was a very satisfying read for at least one African American who was born in 1925, who served in the Rhineland Campaign in France in a black regiment in the U.S. Army commanded by racist white officers over a period which was exactly congruent with that in which Baker served in Italy. As a matter of fact, as I read Baker's account, I checked it against that of the movements of my own 1325th Engineer General Ser-vice Regiment as it followed the advance of the combat units in France and Belgium in December 1944 through May 1945. Ver-non J. Baker's memoir of the participation of his platoon of the 370th Infantry Regiment of the 92d Division, in the Italian cam-paign of the winter of 1944 in World War II, will serve as the definitive account of the black soldier's struggle against the racism of his superior officers while engaging the Germans in combat.

It has been said that a successful memoir universalizes the experience of the author so that a whole class of persons identifies with it. *Lasting Valor*, by Vernon Baker, is an eminent demonstration of this fact. Any black soldier, enlisted man or officer, who served in the U.S. Army between 1944 and 1946 can relate to Baker's experience. Baker was an enlisted man and experienced the cruel racism visited upon black GIs by a racist army. He became an officer and relates how black officers were humiliated by the military. Certainly, any officer can identify with his experiences. His experience with a racist bus driver at Camp Wolters, Texas, is reminiscent of that which Jackie Robinson had, also at an army camp here in the United States.

Baker's modesty, his lingering guilt about the men who were killed on patrols which he led against the Germans and for which he received the Distinguished Service Cross, and his reluctant acceptance of the limelight attendant on his belatedly being awarded the Congressional Medal of Honor all tell us something about him. Nothing in Baker's origins, in his childhood as an orphan in Wyoming, or in his high school experience in Clarinda, Iowa, suggested the career that he would later have as a platoon sergeant and a lieutenant leading combat patrols. On the troop transport taking him and his men to Italy to engage in combat, he comments about his all-black platoon:

> The experience was easily more mystifying for me than for them. I had never spent so much time in close contact with so many black people. During my three years in the segregated Army I had kept to myself as much as possible, uncomfortable with a situation growing up in the rural West did not prepare me for.

At least one other soldier in the U.S. Army had the same sensation in Camp Claiborne, Louisiana, where he felt that the experience of growing up in New York's Hudson Valley ill-prepared him for close contact with a barracks full of black men.

Information in *Lasting Valor* provided an excellent opportunity for me to put my own contemporaneous experience into context. Baker talks of the receding tide against sending blacks to war in 1944. He tells of the resurrection, at Fort Huachuca, Arizona, of the 92d Infantry, the all-black Buffalo Division, and how his old outfit, the 25th Infantry Regiment, was absorbed by the 92d. Of the absorption of the 25th by the 92d, Baker says that the 25th was broken up and the men scattered across a new nonentity, an amalgamation of every black soldier the Army could throw together in one spot. The spirit of the 25th was diluted, Baker says, by the bad actors who were drafted into it.

Baker observes that the 92d Division became what I characterize as a staging area where white officers came, marked a little time, and moved up the ladder. Since white officers weren't dying to command black troops, the officers that they saw at the 92d were not Uncle Sam's brightest and best, he says. Black officers such as himself didn't enjoy any sense of inclusion. They were not consulted. Instead, they were humiliated. If called to division headquarters, black officers were to report to the back door.

Memoirist that I am, the reading of *Lasting Valor* called to mind my situation at Camp Claiborne, Louisiana, where I was stationed in the late spring and early summer of 1944 in the 1325th Engineer General Service Regiment. I worked in regimental headquarters as a battalion sergeant major for the second battalion. Fifty-six years after the fact, I now detect what appears to be a connection between the picture that Baker paints of the events at Fort Huachuca and what I observed in Camp Claiborne at that time. My own assessment of the officers (white) and of the enlisted men (black) of the 1325th Engineers has already been presented in my book *A Brother Like Me: A Memoir* (Queenhyte, 1995) and will not be repeated here, except to say that the situation in the 1325th was worse than that in the 92d. We had no black line officers at all!

At the time that Baker and the 92d Division were arriving in Italy, the 1325th was preparing for deployment to the European Theater of Operations. Replacements were being transferred into the regiment from units on other bases. I recall well that some of these men came from Fort Huachuca and from the 92d Division. I believe that at least one man came from the 370th Infantry. I recall, too, that there was a call for volunteers to go to the infantry. Some men volunteered and left. Quite obviously, what happened was that some of the members of the 92d Division whom Baker characterizes as "bad actors" were transferred to the 1325th Engineers, and volunteers were sought from the latter unit, presumably to replenish the 92d. I also recall that shortly after these events, we had a full-scale riot at Camp Claiborne. Not long after that, the pace of our packing and making ready to move accelerated. In June 1944 the men of the 1325th were going on furlough after basic training, while Baker and his men were in Italy to begin the Italian campaign. The 1325th left Camp Claiborne for Wales in October 1944 and arrived in eastern France some time between Thanksgiving and Christmas of that year. I am not aware that any of us engaged armed enemy soldiers during those bitter cold days of December 1944 in the Rhineland Campaign in eastern France. Nevertheless, Vernon Baker and *Lasting Valor* universalize the experience of black soldiers, enlisted or officer, who served in the U.S. Army in World War II. A gap in the literature of World War II has been filled by this book.

Spotlight on Ron Suskind

Another writer deserving of attention is Ron Suskind, author of *A Hope in the Unseen: An American Odyssey from the Inner City to the Ivy League* (1998), which I reviewed in DOBB. My review of it is repeated here, verbatim.

This is an important book. Though written by a journalist from the Washington bureau of the *Wall Street Journal*, it is not a journalistic work. As this reviewer read it, he was increasingly impressed with the depth to which the author goes in analyzing the person of Cedric Jennings, the young Ballou High School student who is the focus of the book. The same can be said of the treatment which Suskind gives to Barbara Jennings, Cedric's mother. As a matter of fact, I read almost the entire book wondering how this author went about getting these insights into the two of them and into the school and its students. Frankly, until I reached and read the last chapter in *A Hope in the Unseen,* where the author shares technique with us, I was skeptical about the authenticity of the sketches of the two and, in turn, of the degree to which we can rely on the picture we get of this high school in the nation's capital, its faculty, its students, and, indeed, its catchment area. Now, I am not naive. I taught in junior high schools and in high schools in New York City and elsewhere in the 1960s and have some idea of what a terrifying place an inner-city school can be. I recall very well teaching in a junior high school in Brooklyn in 1957 where a minister who came in as a substitute teacher made the comment that the students in that school were "like beasts from hell." Until I read the Suskind book, what I did not realize was that this condition was replicating itself forty years later in other cities and particularly in Washington, D.C.

Ron Suskind's book has the merit of not preaching and of not posing self-righteous questions. What it does do is make one ask oneself questions. Why are the schools so bad in the late 1990s in a city like Washington where blacks are in the majority? Why are the students "like beasts from hell"? How is it that Cedric Jennings, who, Suskind tells us, "is not, by nature, a loner . . . finds himself ever more isolated, walking a gauntlet through the halls, sitting unaccompanied in class, and spending hours in this room"? Why all of this in a school where he is a member of the majority racial group? Why does the principal of Cedric Jennings's high school say of him that he is "too proud" for his own good?

Like Pogo, we have found the enemy and it is us. If it does nothing else, *A Hope in the Unseen* permits us to place blame for conditions which exist in the Frank W. Ballou senior high schools in this nation. The facts suggest very strongly that black people are to blame for the deplorable conditions which exist in these schools in districts where most of us live, whose students, faculty, and administrators up to the level of superintendent are black and in cities whose chief executives are black. Suskind has the grace not to say this, but I cannot escape the conclusion that the blame lies with those who unleash the "beasts from hell" into the schools.

There are compelling inferences to be drawn from Cedric Jennings's experience at Ballou. One is that no person should be required to attend such a school. Certainly no one should be subject to harassment because he strives to excel academically. As Suskind puts it, Cedric is the only male honor student who bears the cross with pride. Put in other terms, the onus of being an achiever is so great at Ballou that only Cedric Jennings is proud of being an honor student. The taunts, threats, and actual assaults that he must bear are sickening. One of the things that comes through very clearly in this book is that large numbers of the present generation of students at Ballou and, by inference, at other inner-city high schools are shockingly belligerent toward their fellows who take academic work seriously. It is hard to see why anyone should be compelled to attend such an institution solely because he lives in its catchment area. Some type of arrangement needs to be worked out to provide alternatives for the Cedric Jenningses of this world. This book should be read by, among others, every administrator who has any responsibility for zoning/placement of students in high schools.

This book could help fuel a trend which was demonstrated in the results of a poll conducted by the Gallup Organization in June 1998 for Phi Delta Kappa, a professional association of educators. These results show that 51 percent of those surveyed favor the use of vouchers to pay tuition at private or church-sponsored schools, while 45 percent oppose it. This is a reversal of opinion over the results of a survey taken in 1996, when 43 percent favored and 54 percent opposed. Perhaps the day is coming when the Cedric Jenningses of this world will not be condemned to an abomination of a high school.

There is at least one instance in which Suskind's analogy is flawed. In speaking of a discount catalog store where Cedric goes with Chiniqua to return a pair of shoes, Suskind characterizes the store as "a branch office of home." The presumption is that this type of store is known to both Chiniqua and Cedric because it is found in low-income areas such as those from which they come. Suskind then goes on to draw an analogy between these types of stores and other "branch offices of home," such as soul-food restaurants. He also writes of "an A.M.E. Baptist church." No such institution exists in America. There is no black Methodist/Baptist denomination in this country. Also, I take issue with Suskind on another count. In mentioning Florida A&M University, a traditionally black university in Tallahassee, Florida, Suskind dismisses it as an engineering school. Florida A&M University is much more than an engineering school. It has achieved eminence for its quality across the disciplines. Suskind passes it over rather summarily.

Lillian Pegues
and *Family Tales: Curse or Happenstance?*

Family Tales: Curse or Happenstance? by Lillian Pegues (Noble House, 1998) is a historical book dealing with the era of the 1860s to which my attention was drawn. Very frankly, I read and reviewed it from a nonfiction perspective. I reprint my online review below.

Lillian Pegues has written an intriguing book which begins with the lives of two slaves, ostensibly her kinfolk. In 1860 they were bought at auction in South Carolina from one of the last consignments of slaves to be shipped there from "the Haitian shores" and were held in slavery on the Pegues Plantation. The book follows the lives of Kwassi and Jessamine and of several of their descendants from then down to current times. Composed of a prologue, fourteen chapters, and an epilogue, this book chronicles the tragedy-filled lives of these achievers. The tales which are told about each of the five generations of the Pegues family unfold against a historical account of events that transpired during the period. The dialog, in almost all cases, attempts the vernacular and the diction of the period. This does not always come off well. As a specialist in nonfiction, this reviewer admittedly brought a nonfiction mind-set to his look at the book. Having said this, I have several observations about this tightly written family history.

It would have been useful to have had some reference made to the sources which the author consulted. I was reminded of a comment attributed to an editor of a manuscript by Truman Capote. That editor wrote in the margin of one of Capote's manuscripts "How know?" I wondered how Dr. Pegues knows some of the things she says about or attributes to Kwassi and Jessamine. The verisimilitude of the work would have been enhanced with a reference, however parenthetical, to her sources.

The persistent invocation of the Obeah man in practically every tale in the book is striking, particularly as regards the current generation of the Pegueses. It is understandable in the case of the generation of Kwassi and Jessamine who lived in the 1860s. It is harder to comprehend as regards those of more recent generations. So too it is with her description of the behavior of the crows that gather on the fences and trees of the plantation and become loud and raucous when tragedy befalls a member of the Pegues family a thousand miles away. Even they, however, "seemed to have prolonged their rituals for a longer period of time as if they were not quite certain just what they should do. It was as if they knew that a very unusual event had occurred, but no one seemed to be sure that they knew just what it was." Could it be that the crows were about their own business, business that had nothing to do with a Pegues?

There are some curious inaccuracies in this book. The most striking is the statement that during the riots of 1967, Justice Thurgood Marshall set up a Commission on Civil Disorders which was chaired by Governor Otto Kerner of Illinois. In the normal course of events, justices of the U.S. Supreme Court do not set up commissions to look into national problems. The fact is that in the late 1960s President Lyndon Baines Johnson established the Kerner Commission to look into urban disorders.

Another inaccuracy is inherent in the account of Winston's separation from the U.S. Navy at the end of World War II. According to Pegues, when his ship arrived back in the United States from the Far East, his separation from the service was instantaneous. As she tells it, Winston collected his gear and said good-bye to all his associates. He purchased a ticket to Steeltown (his home) and was on his way. No one was ever separated from any branch of the U.S. military service in this way. It sounds as if Winston was absent without leave from the moment his ship docked. One asks oneself how to assess the accuracy of the author's recounting of other events which took place long before her birth, when the telling of those which took place well within her lifetime does not inspire confidence regarding their accuracy. But then, a tale is a story or account of true, legendary, or fictitious events. For this reviewer of nonfiction books, the jury is still out as regards the place of *Family Tales: Curse or Happenstance?* in this spectrum.

BEST BOOK LISTS

As the end of the twentieth century neared, many persons and organizations formulated their lists of the best books of the century. Criteria for inclusion in these lists varied from list to list, as well one might expect they would. Consequently, the books that turned up on these lists varied. Two such lists came to my attention. The first, compiled by the journalism department of New York University (NYU), was a list ranking the hundred best works of twentieth-century journalism. The second by Marvin Olasky, a teacher of journalism history at the University of Texas at Austin, was a ten-book list of the best books of the twentieth century. Entitled "I've Got a Little List," it was published in the *Wall Street Journal* on March 12, 1999.

One does not get much insight into the reasons for the inclusion of the books that appear on either list. Since thirty-six persons were involved in the selections on the NYU list, there were probably thirty-six different reasons for each of the books on that list. In the opinion of a *New York Times* reporter, the New York University list focused less on events than on craftsmanship.

MY PERSONAL FAVORITES

One might ask of the "Dunbar on Black Books" best list, "Why are these books on your list of favorites? What criteria did you use to select them?" My list of personal favorites grew out of my special interest in the thinking of the male black intellectual in the late twentieth century. It reflects my strong interest in monitoring the dispersal of the mass of blacks that William Edward Burghardt Du Bois saw in 1903 huddled in the valley under a veil of race. The list reflects the fact that I was, and am, intrigued by the sense of twoness at being black and American that Du Bois claimed was one the hounds of hell that dog blacks in America.

Understandably then, the books on my list of twentieth-century personal favorites are replete with themes, concepts, and credos which had been or have become part of my own social belief system regarding race. Taken together, these constitute an intellectual autobiography or memoir. The books that have found their way onto my list of favorites represent more than a mindless culling of the 907-book "Dunbar on Black Books" canon. Memoirist that I am, some themes that are expressed in these books have resonated in my consciousness for more than fifty years. For me this is a verification of the argument that a successful autobiography or memoir is one in which the author universalizes his or her own experience. Simply put, these books made the cut largely for subjective reasons.

Up from Slavery

Up from Slavery, by Booker T. Washington, and *The Souls of Black Folk,* by W. E. B. Du Bois, published in 1901 and 1903, respectively, are two of my favorite books. They are prisms through which I have looked at the thinking of several other black intellectuals who are products of the second half of the twentieth century and whose books appear on my list of favorites.

Booker T. Washington's *Up from Slavery* has its place on my list because of the regard I came to have for it by reason of its very existence. I was and am impressed with Washington's strong determination to get an education and with his commitment to the education of his people. The difficulties that he overcame and the role that he played in his own education are constantly in my mind when I think of him and his achievements. In point of fact, my sympathy for many of our end-of-the-century youth, who come out of our schools unable to read, is tempered by my recall of what Booker Taliaferro Washington achieved under very difficult circumstances. The stature of this great man can be assessed only through careful reading of his autobiography. This book is *must* reading for those who would understand what is possible against great odds. Marvin Olasky, in his above-cited list, places this book at the number two spot in his ten-book list of the best books of the twentieth century.

The Souls of Black Folk

William Edward Burghardt Du Bois' soliloquy, "Our Spiritual Strivings," that is the first chapter of his *Souls of Black Folk*, sets the scene for those of us who are confessed narcissists who kneel along the stream of literature to attempt to see ourselves reflected in it. In this way we "step within the Veil," raising it so that we may ourselves see its deeper recesses. Du Bois' *Souls of Black Folk* is a work that must be read and reread to be fully appreciated. I read this book for the first time at about age thirty-five. Now thirty-five years and several additional readings later, the significance of this book has become even greater for me. This notwithstanding the fact that I distance myself from Du Bois' views and positions on some issues. The best evidence of the extent to which *The Souls of Black Folk* has withstood the test of time came to the fore in March 1999.

The above-cited study by the journalism department of New York University ranks *The Souls of Black Folk* as number fifteen on its list of the hundred of what it called "journalism's greatest hits" of this century. This book is, to my mind, the best written assessment of the condition of blacks in America at the turn of the last century. (The NYU study also pays tribute to Du Bois in ranking at number ninety-seven a collection of columns that he wrote in *The Crisis Magazine* between 1910 and 1934.)

The Crisis of the Negro Intellectual

The third and fourth books on my list are both there because of the extent to which they relate to the search for self by the male black intellectual in the late twentieth century. At the dawn of the twentieth century Du Bois saw blacks symbolically huddled in a valley under a veil of race. In the post-World War II era I have seen the balkanization of the black masses. While this is true as regards the entire black population, it is particularly evident as regards the intellectual class. My reading of a work by Harold Cruse, a retired black professor at the University of Michigan, called this phenomenon to my attention.

The Crisis of the Negro Intellectual: An Analysis of the Failure of Black Leadership, by Harold Cruse, was first published in 1967. It is a scholarly devastation of the black intellectual, as E. Franklin Frazier's *Black Bourgeoisie* was of the black middle class some ten years earlier. The import of Cruse's book is put in perspective by two of his colleagues at the University of Michigan. In their foreword to the 1984 edition, Bazel E. Allen and Ernest J. Wilson III say it all when they say that it "has established itself as one of the most intellectually provocative and authoritative works of American social criticism published during the tumultuous decade of the 1960s. Unlike so many other controversial books of that politically charged period—expressions of the times rather than analyses of them—Cruse's work provided a model of what could be achieved by black scholars."

This book is an excellent backdrop for the study of the black intellectual's search for self in twentieth-century America. Iconoclast that he is, Cruse has no sacred cows. An example of this is found in his dealing with the subject of black nationalism. At the start of his chapter "Ideology in Black" he tells his readers, "It should not be construed from what has been said thus far that this study is so pro-nationalist it finds only the integrationist wing deserving of criticism." He then goes on to say that the nationalist wing does not know where it is going. Cruse brings his keen mind to bear on every imaginable topic encompassed by the black experience in America. He does so from a state of being well informed on the subjects about which he speaks. One may not agree with him, but one always has the feeling that he has done his homework and has bested you with his arguments because of that. One is left to wonder why we didn't see more of Cruse making these arguments on television in the days of the "Black Revolution." On reflection, I realize that Cruse is more insightful than he is inciting. Incitement was the order of those days.

Christopher Lash, the historian, calls attention to one of the primary characteristics which put Cruse's book on my list of favorites. He said that "when all the manifestoes and polemics of the Sixties are forgotten, this book will survive as a monument of historical analysis."

Reflections of an Affirmative Action Baby

The fourth book on my list of personal favorites is *Reflections of an Affirmative Action Baby,* by Stephen L. Carter (1991.). A few years ago I did a study of black intellectuals in the post-World War II era. I attempted to detect the sense of duality felt by these men at being at the same time black and American. Such a duality, or sense of "twoness," had been identified by W. E. B. DuBois in 1903 and said by him to characterize all blacks. My own effort was to pinpoint expressions of this in the writings of twentieth-century black intellectuals. I hypothesized that the phenomenon persists to the current era. Stephen L. Carter is the first such

product of the second half of this century who came to my attention. *Reflections of an Affirmative Action Baby* comes into the canon of
my favorites because of the thinking that it provides by a contemporary black intellectual about problems that he faces and the
rationales that govern his thinking.

Carter was born in 1954 and is thereby of the generation that
became teenagers during the era of the racial strife of the 1960s.
He was affected, as were other first-rate black students, by the
preferential admissions policies that were adopted by elite institutions. He was admitted to Yale University Law School because
he was black. He became a law professor there because he was
black. His anguish comes from his perception that from high
school in Ithaca, New York, through his college years at Stanford
University, and through Yale Law School, he has been measured
against other blacks, rather than against his entire cohort pool,
irrespective of race.

Carter is in anguish over his position as an intellectual. The
defining characteristic of the intellectual, he says, is not (as some
seem to think) a particular level of educational or cultural attain-
ment and certainly not a particular political stance. His anguish
arises from the fact that he is not just an intellectual but that he
is a *black* intellectual. As such, he must try to foster reconciliation,
to find the common ground, to be at once realistic about the
world and sensitive to others.

Carter's compelling conclusion is that the circumstances that
confront the masses of blacks who have not been privileged is
sufficient reason for those of us who disagree on solutions to
stop fighting each other and seek solutions by actually "talk[ing]
to one another, instead of continuing an endless, self-defeating
argument over who is the authentic keeper of the flame."

To this reviewer Carter's torment seems to be one felt most
by the ablest. They would like to be seen as among the best in
their professions, but that recognition eludes them. Instead they
are told that they are the best black lawyers or the best black doc-

tors or the best black investment bankers, and those who say it consider it a compliment. And, Carter says, "In *this* society, however, we sooner or later must accept that being viewed as the best blacks is part of what has led us to where we are; and we must further accept that to some of our colleagues, black as well as white, we will never be anything else."

This book by an able, clear-thinking black who is committed to improving the lot of his people brings a useful perspective to the affirmative action discussion. The fact that Carter brings a minimum of ideological baggage to the issue is refreshing.

Black Bourgeoisie

The fifth and sixth books on my list are assessments of the black middle class and of the black upper class. *Black Bourgeoisie,* by the eminent black Howard University sociology professor E. Franklin Frazier (1894–1962), was published in English in 1957, after having been published in French in France in 1955. It was the last popular treatment of the black middle class that I can recall and, in any case, the last that I had read before 1999. When I read the book, I was devastated by the depiction of the black middle class which emerged. Frazier characterized the black middle class as being made up of persons living in a world of make-believe that was created by the black press. The black middle class came across as so many who hated themselves and spent every waking moment imitating white people and accepting their values. Quite clearly, Frazier did not consider himself to be a member of this group and stated that he was attacked by leaders in the black community. He said that in one newspaper there was a "sly suggestion" that Negroes should use violence to punish him for being a traitor to the Negro race.

A glance at the chapter titles of the second part of Frazier's book is sufficient to get a feel of the cutting critique of the black bourgeoisie that is contained therein. The title of the second part of the book is "The World of Make-Believe," with one chapter given over to "Negro Business: A Social Myth." Frazier starts with the premise that the capital investment represented by Negro business is insignificant. He then sets about to show that a social myth had been fabricated by Negroes around Negro business to "compensate for its feeling of inferiority in a white world dominated by business enterprise." He attributes the creation of this myth to "a small group of Negro intellectuals and Negro leaders who accepted racial separation as the inevitable solution of the race problem."

The chapter on "The Negro Press and Wish-Fulfillment" is another haymaker, this one aimed at the Negro intellectual. Frazier, in a left-handed compliment, says, "The Negro press is . . . one of the most successful business enterprises owned and controlled by Negroes." He continues with the following hard right, "It [the Negro press] is the chief medium of communication which creates and perpetuates the world of make-believe for the black bourgeoisie." All of this comes together in Frazier's reasoning that the black press with its exaggerations concerning the economic well-being and cultural achievements of Negroes, and its emphasis on Negro "society," creates a world of make-believe into which the black bourgeoisie can escape from its inferiority and inconsequence in American society. This leads into the most devastating of Frazier's onslaughts.

In the chapter entitled " 'Society': Status without Substance," Professor Frazier delivers his most painful body blows to the black middle class. As a matter of fact, the argument could be made that this chapter is the blow that knocked out the black middle class of the post-World War II era.

Our Kind of People

I believe that the black middle class, as portrayed by Frazier, has been "out of it" for the forty years between the publication of

Black Bourgeoisie in 1957 and the publication of the sixth book on my list. I also believe that Frazier's attack and that of the black militants of the sixties on middle-class blacks forced the latter into virtual hiding. Enter Lawrence Otis Graham and *Our Kind of People: Inside America's Black Upper Class* (HarperCollins, 1999).

Lawrence Otis Graham has written an unapologetic book proudly heralding not the rebirth of the black middle class but the birth of its successor—the black upper class. This group does not suffer the lack of a feeling of self-worth, nor does it live the marginalized social life vis-à-vis white America that characterized the group described by Frazier. The members of the group portrayed by Graham are real players.

Graham, a black Harvard-educated lawyer, unlike Frazier, is a proud member of the black upper class. He has thus been able to observe this group across the country because of his considerable contacts, including relatives. The more than six years which he gave to writing the book and the more than three hundred persons that he interviewed and/or consulted lend credibility to his work.

Our Kind of People is an anecdotal study of upper-class black Americans in several American cities where cohort groups of such people exist—people whose roots can be traced back almost four hundred years, Graham tells us. The black upper class he portrays is a self-defined group. This is one of the things that distinguishes Graham's technique from that used by Frazier in *Black Bourgeoisie.* Frazier, who quite obviously did not see himself as a member of the class of people he was studying, adapted sociological techniques to the study of people who were alien to his own spirit. Graham, on the other hand, has taken a group to which he has an affinity and let its members define themselves. Graham makes no apology for the elitist mind-set of the black upper class. The result is a book that is not just a good read but a fascinating one.

Several criteria, in varying degrees, seem to figure in determining who is or is not in the black upper class. Wealth, type of home, education, skin color, lineage, intelligence, social skills, presentability of spouse and offspring, self-confidence, and profession are among them.

Length of time during which a prospect's forebears have been in the upper class is also a consideration. The evidence suggests, however, that around the country there is flexibility exercised in the application of each of these criteria. It seems clear that only those who are said to be members by the local arbiters of the subject are indeed members. Membership in certain church denominations and social organizations are *de rigueur* in being selected for membership in the black upper class. The names that surface in this book constitute a registry of the black upper class from its inception to current times.

Membership in certain fraternal organizations is a criterion which is emphasized in *Our Kind of People.* Consequently, the role which Alpha Phi Alpha Fraternity, Inc., enjoys in the election of prospects into this aristocracy of race and culture is of great interest to those of us who are Alphas. First, we are told that the membership of this fraternity, founded at Cornell in 1906, is "a veritable who's who in black America."

Many among those who Graham characterizes as the old-guard black elite "would argue that only three of the fraternities—the Alphas, the Kappas, and the Omegas—actually fit the 'society' profile." His own father-in-law who pledged Alpha in 1947 told him that an Alpha man is "the nice guy—that everyone wants his sister to date." Graham, in a poignant passage, regrets that his Princeton experience precluded his becoming a member of a fraternity, black or otherwise. He tells us that "I have long felt alien to—and envious of—the experience that my friends received at other colleges." What he felt that he missed was the experience of being inducted as a college student into a black Greek-letter organization. It is clear that he would have been interested in admission to Alpha Phi Alpha Fraternity, which he characterizes as the best of them all.

Men of Alpha are prominent among those whom Graham cites, quotes, interviews, and otherwise features in this book. We are left with the clear impression that men of Alpha are, in their own right, "our kind of people." Consequently, it was very easy for this reviewer to insinuate himself vicariously into the company of the personalities that Graham profiles here.

J. Raymond Jones, the 1940s political operative in Harlem, was once told what an opposing black, a Harvard-educated politician, had said about him, to which Jones replied that Harvard had ruined more blacks than bad whiskey. J. Raymond Jones would think that the notion of an upper-class black is the conception of a ruined mind. Some of those who are of Graham's cohort group see the situation differently than he does. Each reader will bring his or her own experience to the reading of *Our Kind of People: Inside America's Black Upper Class.* Those of us who have been ruined by the bad whiskey of a black fraternity or sorority experience will come down in one place. Those who have not experienced the debilitating drafts of elitism will come down in another. No matter which group the reader belongs to, he or she will find this book insightful.

Kafka Was the Rage

Four additional books complete my list of ten favorites. *Kafka Was the Rage: A Greenwich Village Memoir,* by Anatole Broyard (Vintage, 1997), is a significant book in the study of the black intellectual and the twoness he feels at being at once an American and a black. Broyard solved the problem in a manner that is not available to the majority of us. He served in the U.S. Army during World War II as a white man. He was a commissioned officer in an all-black stevedore battalion. Around 1946, when he returned from service, Broyard left his black wife and child in the Bedford-Stuyvesant section of Brooklyn and went to live as a white man in Greenwich Village. This book, which was published posthumously, chronicles the largely cerebral life which he led.

Thirteen Ways of Looking at a Black Man

The next book, *Thirteen Ways of Looking at a Black Man,* by Henry Louis Gates, Jr. (Random House, 1997), is significant in connection with my Anatole Broyard study. In it, Gates profiles Broyard, along with such people as James Baldwin, Romare Bearden, Harry Belafonte, Eldridge Cleaver, Ralph Ellison, Louis Farrakhan, Bill T. Jones, Albert Murray, and Colin Powell. He talked with others such as Josephine Baker and Spike Lee in developing these profiles. Gates adds perspective to each of these well-known figures by eliciting information from them which this reviewer had not found in previous works dealing with them. It is thus that we learn much about Anatole Broyard that we are not able to get from other sources, *Kafka Was the Rage* included. In instances where he broached sensitive issues in his interviews with profilees, Gates was obviously rewarded with candor and honesty. One wonders what might have been the outcome had he been able to interview Anatole Broyard before the latter's death.

The fact that Gates had not interviewed Broyard for "The Passing of Anatole Broyard" does not make the piece any less insightful for this reviewer. The fact that it turns on the very familiar axis of the A-line of the Independent subway system between the Bedford-Stuyvesant section of Brooklyn where I lived and Greenwich Village where I attended NYU from 1946 to 1949 is relevant for this memoirist. Gates' quote of Wilmer Lucas, Broyard's black friend from Bed-Stuy, is also relevant. (I remember Lucas as a fellow student in the late 1940s at the NYU

Washington Square Center in the Village.) Gates quotes the now–University of Tennessee professor as saying of Broyard, "He was black when he got on the subway in Brooklyn, but as soon as he got out at West Fourth Street he became white." This documents Gates' attribution to Broyard of the notion of race as "an elective option." Gates' skillful profile of Anatole Broyard in and of itself merits this book's being listed as one of my top ten favorites.

Colored People

Another book on my list, *Colored People: A Memoir,* also by Henry Louis Gates, Jr. (Alfred A. Knopf, 1994), is, to my mind, an exemplar of what one hopes is a prototype of a twenty-first-century black intellectual prepared to civilly coexist with people who are different from him. Having known the hurt that comes from a childhood in an environment of enforced separation by race, Gates says in a letter to his children,

> I rebel at the notion that I can't be part of other groups, that I can't construct identities through elective affinity, that race must be the most important thing about me. Is that what I want on my gravestone: Here lies an African American? So I'm divided. I want to be black, to know black, to luxuriate in whatever I might be calling my blackness at any particular time—but to do so in order to come out the other side, to experience a humanity that is neither colorless nor reducible to color.

To this reviewer this message seems destined as much for those blacks who take issue with Henry Louis Gates about his views on race as it is for his children. The tenor of this book and its message commend it to this list of favorites.

Out of America

The last book on my list, *Out of America: A Black Man Confronts Africa*, by Keith B. Richburg (1998), on which I have previously commented at length, rounds out my list. It could prove to be a watershed phenomenon as regards the current romanticism with which some African Americans relate to our African ancestry and heritage. Perhaps more African-American writers will come to recognize the irrelevance of our African ancestry in confronting the problems we face in trying to survive and achieve in the American environment.

PERSONAL FULFILLMENT

The volume that I have selected to close out this bibliomemoir is a most significant one. In a sense, *The History of Alpha Phi Alpha: A Development in College Life*, by Charles H. Wesley (Foundation Publishers, seventeenth printing, 2000, limited edition), is the end volume, both literally and metaphorically, on my personal afroimprint bookshelf. With W. E. B. Du Bois' *Souls of Black Folk* on the metaphorical left and about fifteen books in between, books that I have made part of myself through unceasing reference over my adult professional life, Charles H. Wesley's book is the end volume on the right.

As a reader since childhood—a reader whose reading has shaped his perspective in many ways—I have only lately come to recognize the extent to which this shaping has occurred. As Colin Powell said, one learns much about himself in writing his memoirs. It is no doubt obvious to readers who have reached this point in this book that I have internalized much of my reading. I have said again and again that I did and continue to do this with Du Bois' work and with that of others. I stare into the stream of literature to find my reflection. I insinuate myself into the context. Thus my connection to Charles H. Wesley and the history of Alpha Phi Alpha Fraternity, Inc.

I was initiated into Eta Chapter of Alpha Phi Alpha Fraternity, Inc., in New York City in 1948 while I was an undergraduate student at New York University. Included among the materials I was given after this rite was a copy of the fifth edition of *The History of Alpha Phi Alpha: A Development in College Life*, by Charles H. Wesley, which Dr. Wesley had revised that very year. I read it carefully, and I still have it on my bookshelf, along with a copy of the sixteenth edition which was published in 1996, after his death.

Over the years from 1965 through the year 2000, as a delegate representing my local chapter in Rockland County, New York, I have attended every national convention of Alpha Phi Alpha Fraternity. These meetings are held annually in cities across the country. Past conventions have been held in such cities as Anaheim, Atlanta, Chicago, Cleveland, Dallas, Detroit, Houston, Los Angeles, Miami, Minneapolis, New York, Philadelphia, San Antonio, and St. Louis. In some instances I served on convention committees and got to know many influential members of the brotherhood. As a young college teacher I came to have great respect for Dr. Wesley as I observed him making presentations at these meetings. Further, I had the occasion to learn of his scholarly writings outside of Alpha Phi Alpha Fraternity.

In January 1997 I attended the inaugural convocation of Adrian Wallace in New Orleans where he was installed as the thirtieth general president of Alpha Phi Alpha Fraternity. At a reception there, while I was sampling finger food, Brother Wallace walked up to me and said quietly that he was appointing me chairman of the Publications Committee. Needless to say I was astounded, delighted, and humbled and consented to serve. In this capacity, I consulted with the editor in chief of the official fraternity organ,

The Sphinx, and reviewed all Alpha Phi Alpha Fraternity publications and reported my findings and recommendations to the next convention. At the invitation of the editor in chief of *The Sphinx*, I wrote reviews of several nonfiction books, which were published on a regular basis in volumes 84 and 85.

Early in 1999, President Wallace appointed a Historical Commission and appointed me to it. The commission consisted of the following members of the fraternity: Dr. Thomas D. Pawley III, a professor emeritus of Lincoln University in Jefferson City, Missouri; Dr. Julius E. Thompson, director of the Black Studies Program and associate professor in the Department of History at the University of Missouri at Columbia; Dr. Clint C. Wilson, II, professor of journalism at Howard University; Dr. Joseph T. Durham, president emeritus of the Baltimore Community College; Myron Rodney Robinson, of Hyattsville, Maryland; and Seaton J. White, the editor in chief of *The Sphinx*. Ronald L. Anderson, then Executive Director of Alpha Phi Alpha, was appointed ex-officio. President Wallace sits ex-officio on the commission. He appointed Dr. Robert L. Harris, Jr., a professor of African-American history at Cornell University, as historian of the fraternity and chairman of the Historical Commission.

This environment immediately catalyzed my interest in book publishing. I say this because at its first meeting President Wallace charged the commission, among other things, with the responsibility (1) for preparing a final edition of the Wesley history book and (2) for preparing a second edition of the history of Alpha Phi Alpha Fraternity, documenting the closing out of its twentieth-century history, to be in print before the fraternity's centennial in 2006. The net result of all of this was that I found myself catapulted into a book publishing environment, since as chairman of the Publications Committee I had responsibility for oversight of all publications and as a member of the Historical

Commission I sat on what is virtually the board of directors of Foundation Publishers. I thoroughly enjoy holding these positions, and it was to get even better sooner rather than later.

As fraternity historian, Dr. Harris began to conceptualize the span of time that the final edition of the Wesley history should cover. After consulting with the members of the commission, he decided that he would add to the book a Chapter 20, entitled "Social Purpose and Social Action," bringing the history up to the year 1976. That year had been marked by Alpha Phi Alpha's first international convention which was held in Monrovia, Liberia. That was also the last year of the administration of Dr. Walter Washington as president of Alpha and was the nation's bicentennial year. Dr. Harris observes in the chapter that he has added to the book that the delegation to the Alpha Phi Alpha convention in Liberia was "the largest contingent of black Americans to travel to the African continent except during wartime." Dr. Harris decided that the final edition of the Wesley history should close with an epilogue in tribute to the venerable Dr. Charles H. Wesley. He asked me to write it, and I did so.

A limited, 1000-copy, leather-bound edition of the seventeenth printing of *The History of Alpha Phi Alpha: A Development in College Life,* by Dr. Charles H. Wesley, with an update by Dr. Robert L. Harris, Jr., and an epilogue by Dr. Harry B. Dunbar, went on sale in the "Alpha Store" in the Convention Exhibit Hall of the Hyatt Regency Atlanta Hotel on Saturday, August 5, 2000. Six of the seven living past general presidents of Alpha Phi Alpha Fraternity, Inc., were present. They included the twenty-fifth, James R. Williams; the twenty-sixth, Ozell Sutton; the twenty-seventh, Charles C. Teamer, Sr.; the twenty-eighth, Henry Ponder; the twenty-ninth, Milton C. Davis; and the incumbent, the thirtieth, Adrian L. Wallace. They autographed books for those who wished to have them do so. The historian and the author of the epilogue also obliged those who asked. The fact is not lost on me that the seventeenth edition was presented to the convention in the city of Atlanta seventy-one years after Charles H. Wesley had presented the first in the same city in 1929.

This book is and will forever be a monument to my fulfillment as a member of Alpha Phi Alpha Fraternity for fifty-two years, as an author, as a publishing consultant, and indeed as a publisher. Moreover, the Alpha Phi Alpha Meritorious Service Award, a beautiful clear-plastic, flame-shaped standing plaque which was presented to me in August 2000 in recognition of my contribution to the fraternity's publications, is a humbling tribute. Through it I have been etched not only into the history of Alpha Phi Alpha but into that of the afroimprint.

Appendix A

References

PRINT

Alexander, Amy. 1999. "One Smart Publisher!" *Black Issues Book Review* (September–October): p. 47.

Bader, Barbara. 1997. "History Changes Color." *The Horn Book Magazine* (January 11), as cited in *Electric Library.*

Black Issues Book Review. 1999. "The African American Century 100 Years of Pioneering Achievements" (November–December): pp. 33–52.

————. 1999. "Self-Publishing" (September–October 1999) p. 48.

Carney, Vaughn A. 1996. "Publishing's Ugly Obsession." *Wall Street Journal* (June 17).

Electric Library, as cited from Africa News Service. 1998. "Pan-Africanist without Peer Dubois: Man of the Century" (October 5).

Jacques, Geoffrey "Readers Look for Answers in Works of History, Faith and Imagination." *Publishers Weekly* (December 9, 1996)

McG. Thomas, Jr., Robert. 1998. "Daisy Anderson, 97, Widow of Former 'Slave and Union Soldier.' " *New York Times* (September 26).

Pawley, Thomas D. 1999. "Historical Moment: The Foundation Publishers, A Subsidiary of Alpha Phi Alpha Fraternity, Inc." *The Sphinx* (vol. 84, no. 2), pp. 67–68.

Reed, Ishmael. 1999. "Our Future Is Cyberspace." *Black Issues Book Review* (November–December): p. 51.

The Sphinx. 1998. "Former New York City Black Panther Becomes Leading Mississippi Businessman" (vol. 83, no. 1): pp. 15–17.

WEBSITES

Amber Books:
www.amberbooks.com

Dunbar on Black Books:
www.netword.com/Harry B. Dunbar

Genesis Press:
www.genesis-press.com

Howard University archives:
www.founders.howard.edu/huarchivesnet/0002huarnet
/current.htm

Publishers Catalog Home Page (directory of over 7000 publishers):
www.lights.com/publisher

University of North Carolina at Chapel Hill Academic Library project "Documenting the American South" ("The Church in the Southern Black Community: Bibliography" is located at this site.):
docsouth.unc.edu

PART TWO

DUNBAR BLACK
BOOK BIBLIOGRAPHY

A Legacy from
the Twentieth Century

Abdul-Jabbar, Kareem, with Alan Steinberg. 1996. *Black Profiles in Courage: A Legacy of African-American Achievement.* Morrow. ISBN 0-6881309-7-6.

Abernathy, Donzaleigh, and Robert F. Kennedy, Jr. 1998. *Partners to History: Martin Luther King, Ralph Abernathy and the Civil Rights Movement.* General Publishing Group. ISBN 1575440-7-4.

Abner, Allison, and Linda Villarosa. 1998. *The Black Parenting Book: Caring for Our Children in the First Five Years.* Broadway Books. ISBN 0-7679019-6-7.

Abu-Jamal, Mumia. 2001. *All Things Censored.* Seven Stories Press. ISBN 1-5832202-2-4.

Adams, Janus. 1998. *Freedom Days: 365 Inspired Moments in Civil Rights History.* John Wiley. ISBN 0-4712910-4-8.

Adams, Michael Vannoy. 1996. *The Multicultural Imagination: "Race," Color and the Unconscious.* Routledge. ISBN 0-4151383-8-8.

Adeleke, Tunde. 1998. *Unafrican Americans: Nineteenth-Century Black Nationalists and the Civilizing Mission.* University Press of Kentucky. ISBN 0-8131-2056-x.

Aghahowa, Brenda Eatman. 1996. *Praising in Black and White: Unity and Diversity in Christian Worship.* Pilgrim Press/United Press Church. ISBN 0-8298113-4-6.

Alexander, Amy. 1997. *The Farrakhan Factor: African American Writers on Leadership, Nationhood, and Minister Louis Farrakhan.* Introduction by Henry Louis Gates, Jr. Grove Press. ISBN 0-8021-1623-x.

Alexander, Lydia Lewis, et al. 1998. *Wearing Purple.* Crown/Harmony. ISBN 0-6098017-4-0.

Alexander, M. Jacqui, L. Albrecht, et al. 1997. *The Third Wave: Feminists Perspectives on Racism.* Kitchen Table: Women of Color Press. ISBN 0-91315-25-0.

Ali, Alfred. 1995. *Sixty-Four Years to Make a Negro! Willie Lynch Speech to the American Slave-Owners of 1712.* Alfred Ali Literary Works. ISBN 0-963-6025-3-5.

Allen, Marcus, with Carlton Stowers. 1997. *Marcus: The Autobiography of Marcus Allen.* St. Martin's Press. ISBN 0-312-16924-8.

Allen, Theodore W. 1997. *The Invention of the White Race.* Volume Two: *The Origins of Racial Oppression in Anglo-America.* Verso. ISBN 1-85984-9814.

Allen, Will, and Daniel Murray In press. *Banneker: The Afro American Astronomer.* Black Classic Press. ISBN 0-933121-48-2.

Ambrose, Stephen F. 1999. *Citizen Soldiers: The U.S. Army from the Normandy Beaches to the Bulge to the Surrender of Germany, June 7, 1944–May 7, 1945.* Diane Publishing Company. ISBN 0-7881605-0-8.

America, Richard F., and Bernard E. Anderson. 1996. *Soul in Management: How African-American Managers Can Succeed in a White Business Environment.* Birch Lane. ISBN 1-55972-353-X.

Amos, Wally, and Stu Glauberman. 1996. *Watermelon Magic: Seeds of Wisdom, Slices of Life.* Beyond Words Publishing. ISBN 1-8852234-7-1.

Anderson, Claud. 1994. *Black Labor, White Wealth: The Search for Power and Economic Justice.* Duncan & Duncan Publishers. ISBN 1-878647-11-3.

Anderson, Elijah. 1999. *Code of the Street: Decency, Violence and the Moral Life of the Inner City.* Norton. ISBN 0-393-04023-2.

Anderson, Jervis. 1997. *Bayard Rustin: Troubles I've Seen.* Harper-Collins. ISBN 0-0601670-2-5.

Anderson, S. E. 1995. *The Black Holocaust for Beginners.* Writers and Readers. ISBN 0-86316-178-2.

Andrews, William L., et al., eds. 1997. *The Oxford Companion to African American Literature.* Oxford University Press. ISBN 0-19-506510-7.

Angelou, Maya. 1998. *Even the Stars Look Lonesome.* Random House. ISBN 0-553-37972-0.

Appiah, K. Anthony, and Henry Louis Gates, Jr. eds. 1999. *Africana: The Encyclopedia of the African and African American Experience.* Basic/Civitas. ISBN 0-4650007-1-1.

Appiah, K. Anthony, and Amy Gutmann. 1996. *Color Conscious: The Political Morality of Race.* Princeton University Press. ISBN 0-691-02661-0.

Applebome, Peter. 1996. *Dixie Rising: How the South Is Shaping American Values Politics, and Culture.* Crown. ISBN 0-8129-26536.

Archibald, Chestina Mitchell. 1997. *Say Amen: The African American Family's Book of Prayers.* New American Library. ISBN 0-525-94215-7.

Armour, Jody David. 1997. *Negrophobia and Reasonable Racism: The Hidden Costs of Being Black in America.* New York University Press. ISBN 0-8147064-0-1.

Asante, Molefe Kete. 1998. *The Afrocentric Idea.* Temple University Press. ISBN 1-5663959-4-1.

Ashmore, Harry. 1997. *Civil Rights and Wrongs: A Memoir of Race and Politics, 1944–1996.* University of South Carolina Press. ISBN 1-5700318-7-8.

Astor, Gerald. 1998. *The Right to Fight: A History of African Americans in the Military.* Presidio Press. ISBN 0-89141-632-3.

Avery, Byllye. 1999. *An Altar of Words: Wisdom, Comfort and Inspiration for African American Women.* Broadway Books. ISBN 0-7679008-0-4.

Ayittey, George B. N. 1997. *Africa in Chaos.* St. Martin's Press. ISBN 0-3121640-0-9.

Azoulay, Katya Gibel. 1997. *Black, Jewish, and Interracial.* Duke University Press. ISBN 0-8223197-1-3.

Bak, Richard. 1998. *Joe Louis: The Great Black Hope.* Da Capo Press. ISBN 0-3068087-9-x.

Bakari, Rosenna. 1995. *Self Love: Developing and Maintaining Self-Esteem for the Black Woman.* Karibu Publishing. ISBN 0-9642744-3-4.

Baker, T. Lindsy, and Julia P. Baker. 1997. *Till Freedom Cried Out: Memories of Texas Slave Life.* Texas A&M University Press. ISBN 0-8909673-6-9.

Baker, Vernon, with Ken Olsen. 1999. *Lasting Valor.* Genesis Press. ISBN 1-8854785-1-8.

Baldwin, James. 1998. *Collected Essays: Notes of a Native Son, Nobody Knows My Name, The Fire Next Time, No Name in the Street, The Devil Finds Work, Other Essays.* Edited by Toni Morrison. Library of America. ISBN 1-8830115-2-3.

Ball, Edward. 2000. *Slaves in the Family.* Ballantine Publishing Group. ISBN 0-3459176-3-4.

Ball, Howard. 1999. *A Defiant Life: Thurgood Marshall and the Persistence of Racism in America.* Crown. ISBN 0-5175993-1-7.

Banks, Jr., William H. 1996. *Black Intellectuals: Race and Responsibility in American Life.* Norton. ISBN 0-3930198-9-7.

———. 1996. *The Black Muslims.* Chelsea House Publishers. ISBN 0-7910-2594-2.

Bannerman, Helen. 1996. *The Story of Little Babaji.* HarperCollins. ISBN 0-0620506-5-6.

Baraka, Amiri [LeRoi Jones]. 1997. *Autobiography of LeRoi Jones.* Chicago Review Press. ISBN 1-55652-231-2.

———. 1997. *Jesse Jackson and Black People.* Third World Press. ISBN 0-88378-159-x.

———. 1998. *Home: Social Essays.* HarperCollins. ISBN 0-8800157-2-1.

Barboza, Steven, ed. 1998. *The African American Book of Values.* Doubleday. ISBN 0-3854825-9-0.

Barkun, Michael. 1996. *Religion and the Racist Right: The Origins of the Christian Identity Movement.* University of North Carolina Press. ISBN 0-8078463-8-4.

Barras, Jonetta Rose. 2000. *Whatever Happened to Daddy's Little Girl? The Impact of Fatherlessness on Black Women.* One World. ISBN 0-3454224-6-5.

Barrett, Paul M. 2000. *The Good Black: A True Story of Race in America.* Dutton/Plume. ISBN 0-4522785-9-7.

Bascom, Lionel, ed. 2001. *A Renaissance in Harlem: Lost Voices of an American Community.* HarperTrade. ISBN 0-3807990-2-2.

Bates, Karen, and Karen Hudson. 1997. *Basic Black: Home Training for Modern Times.* Doubleday. ISBN 0-6142535-2-7.

Battle, Stafford L., and Ray O. Harris. 1996. *The African American Resource Guide to the Internet and Online Service.* McGraw-Hill. ISBN 0-0700549-9-1.

Bauman, Mark K., and Berkley Kalin, eds. 1997. *The Quiet Voices: Southern Rabbis and Black Civil Rights, 1880s to 1990s.* University of Alabama Press. ISBN 0-8173089-2-x.

Baxter, Freddie Mae. 1999. *The Seventh Child: A Lucky Life.* Alfred A. Knopf. ISBN 0-3754062-0-4.

Beckwith, Francis J., and Todd Edwin Jones, eds. 1997. *Affirmative Action: Social Justice or Reverse Discrimination?* Prometheus Books. ISBN 1-5739215-7-2.

Belkin, Lisa. 2000. *Show Me a Hero: A Tale of Murder, Suicide, Race and Redemption.* Little Brown. ISBN 0-3160886-4-1.

Bell, Derrick. 1996. *Gospel Choirs: Psalms of Survival in an Alien Land Called Home.* Basic Books. ISBN 0-465-02412-2.

——. 1997. *Afrolantica Legacies.* Third World Press. ISBN 0-8837819-9-9.

Bell, Geneva. 1997. *My Rose: An African American Mother's Story of AIDS.* United Church Press. ISBN 0-8298116-0-5.

BelMonte, Kathryn I. 1998. *African American Heroes and Heroines: 150 True Stories of Black American Heroism.* Lifetime Books. ISBN 081190890.

Belton, Don, ed. 1997. *Speak My Name. Black Men on Masculinity and the American Dream.* Beacon Press. ISBN 0-8070093-7-7.

Bennett, Lerone. 1964. *The Negro Mood and Other Essays.* Johnson Publishing Company. ISBN 0-8748501-2-6.

Berger, Maurice. 1999. *White Lies: Race and the Myths of Whiteness.* Farrar, Straus & Giroux. ISBN 0-3742894-9-2.

Bergmann, Barbara R. 1997. *In Defense of Affirmative Action.* Basic Books. ISBN 0-4650983-4-7.

Bergreen, Laurence. 1997. *Louis Armstrong: An Extravagant Life.* Ivan R. Dee. ISBN 1-56663-157-2.

Berlin, Ira. 1998. *Many Thousands Gone: The First Two Centuries of Slavery in North America.* Harvard University Press. ISBN 0-6748109-2-9.

Berlin, Ira, Marc Favreau, and Steven F. Miller. 1998. *Remembering Slavery: African Americans Talk about Their Personal Experiences of Slavery and Emancipation.* New Press. ISBN 1-56584-425-4.

Berlin, Ira, and Leslie S. Rowland. 1998. *Families and Freedom: A Documentary History of African-American Kinship in the Civil War Era.* New Press. ISBN 1-56584-440-8.

Berman, Paul, ed. 1996. *Blacks and Jews: Alliances and Arguments.* Oxford University Press. ISBN 0-6141288-2-x.

Berrett, Joshua. 1999. *The Louis Armstrong Companion: Eight Decades of Commentary.* Music Sales Corporation. ISBN 0-0286466-9-x.

Berry, Barbara Cochran. 1995. *Life after Johnnie Cochran.* Basic Books. ISBN 0-4650396-5-0.

Bickley, Dan. 1997. *No Bull: The Unauthorized Biography of Dennis Rodman.* St. Martin's Press. ISBN 0-3121711-9-6.

Billingsley, Andrew. 1999. *Mighty Like a River: The Black Church and Social Reform.* Oxford University Press. ISBN 0-1951061-7-2.

Blackburn, Robin. 1997. *The Making of New World Slavery: From the Baroque to the Modern, 1492–1800.* Verso. ISBN 1-8598489-0-7.

Blake, Jody. 1999. *Le Tumulte Noir: Modernist Art and Popular Entertainment in Jazz-Age Paris, 1900–1930.* Penn State Press. ISBN 0-2710175-3-8.

Bogle, Donald. 1997. *Dorothy Dandridge: A Biography.* HarperTrade. ISBN 1-5674303-4-1.

Bolden, Tonya. 1996. *The Book of African-American Women.* Adams Media Corporation. ISBN 1-5585064-7-0.

Bolden, Tonya. 1998. *And Not Afraid to Dare: The Stories of Ten African-American Women.* Scholastic Press. ISBN 059048084.

———. 1999. *Strong Men Keep Coming: The Book of African American Men.* John Wiley. ISBN 0-4713487-3-2.

Bolen, II, David B. 1995. *The Essence of Living: Reaching beyond Global Insanity.* New Verity Publishing. ISBN 0-9641909-0-7.

———. 1997. *How You See It How You Don't: Discover the Magic and Power of Your Own Beliefs.* New Verity Publishing. ISBN 0-9641909-1-5.

Bolick, Clint. 1996. *The Affirmative Action Fraud. Can We Restore the American Civil Rights Vision?* Cato Institute. ISBN 1-8825772-7-2.

Bolster, W. Jeffrey. 1998. *Black Jacks: African American Seamen in the Age of Sail.* Harvard University Press. ISBN 0-6740762-7-3.

Bontemps, Arna, and Langston Hughes. 1997. *The Pasteboard Bandit.* Oxford University Press. ISBN 0-1951147-6-0.

Boston, Kelvin. 1997. *Smart Money Moves for African-Americans.* Berkley Publishing Group. ISBN 0-3995226-2-X.

Boulais, Sue. 1998. *Vanessa Williams: Saving the Best for Last.* Mitchell Lane Publishers. ISBN 1-8838457-5-0.

Bowman, Rob. 1997. *Soulsville, USA: The Stax Records Story.* Music Sales Corporation. ISBN 0-8256722-7-9.

Bowser, Pearl, and Louise Spencer. 2000. *Writing Himself into History: Oscar Micheaux, His Silent Films, and His Audience.* Rutgers University Press. ISBN 0-8135280-2-x.

Boyd, Herb. 1995. *The Black Black Panthers for Beginners.* Writers and Readers. ISBN 0-86316-196-0.

———, ed. 2001. *Autobiography of a People: Three Centuries of African American History Told by Those Who Lived It.* Vintage Anchor Publishing. ISBN 0-3854927-9-0.

Boyd, Julia A. 1997. *Embracing the Fire: Sisters Talk about Sex and Relationships.* New American Library. ISBN 0-525-93959-8.

Boyd, Todd Edward. 1997. *Am I Black Enough for You? Popular Culture from the 'Hood and Beyond.* Indiana University Press. ISBN 0-2533324-2-7.

Boyer, Karl P. 1993. *A Resource Directory of Famous African Americans and Organizations.* Positive and Black. ISBN 0-9642154-0-3.

Boykin, Keith. 1996. *One More River to Cross: Black and Gay in America.* Anchor. ISBN 0-385-47982-4.

Boyle, Sheila Tully, and Andrew Bunnie. 2001. *Paul Robeson: The Years of Promise and Achievement.* University of Massachusetts Press. ISBN 1-5584914-9-x.

Braden, Warren R. 1999. *Homies: Peer Mentoring among African-American Males.* Educational Studies Press. ISBN 1-8795281-4-2.

Bradshaw, English. 1996. *Lifting the Veil.* Duncan & Duncan Publishers. ISBN 0-6141627-3-4.

———. 1996. *My Father's Business.* Duncan & Duncan Publishers. ISBN 1-8877980-3-x.

Bragg, Janet Harmon, with Marjorie M. Kriz. 1996. *Soaring above Setbacks: The Autobiography of Janet Harmon Bragg, African American Aviator.* Smithsonian Institution Press. ISBN 1-56098-458-9.

Branch, Shelly. 1997. *Dollar Pinching: A Consumer's Guide to Smart Spending.* Warner Books. ISBN 0-4466724-6-7.

Branch, Taylor. 1989. *Parting the Waters: America in the King Years, 1954–63.* Simon & Schuster. ISBN 0-6716874-2-5.

———. 1999. *Pillar of Fire: America in the King Years, 1963–65.* Simon & Schuster. ISBN 0-6848480-9-0.

Brandt, Eric, ed. 2000. *Dangerous Liaisons: Blacks and Gays and the Struggle for Equality.* New Press. ISBN 1-56584-455-6.

Brandt, Nat. 1996. *Harlem at War: The Black Experience in WW II.* Syracuse University. ISBN 0-8156-0324-X.

Bray, Rosemary L. 1999. *Unafraid of the Dark: A Memoir.* Doubleday. ISBN 0-3854947-5-0.

Britton, Crystal. 1996. *African-American Art.* Smithmark Publishers. ISBN 0-7651995-2-1.

Brode, Douglas. 1996. *Denzel Washington: His Films and Career.* Carol Publishing Group. ISBN 1-5597238-1-5.

Brodkin, Karen. 1999. *How Jews Became White Folks and What That Says about Race in America.* Rutgers University Press. ISBN 0-8135258-9-6.

Brookman, Philip. 1998. *Gordon Parks.* Little Brown. ISBN 0-8212255-1-0.

Brooks, Gwendolyn. 1996. *Report from Part Two.* Third World Press. ISBN 0-88378-162-x.

Brooks, Roy L. 1999. *Integration or Segregation? A Strategy for Racial Equality.* Harvard University Press. ISBN 0-6744564-5-9.

Broussard, Cheryl D. 1996. *The Black Woman's Guide to Financial Independence.* Penguin. ISBN 0-14-025283-5.

———. 1997. *Sister CEO: The Black Woman's Guide to Starting Your Own Business.* Viking Penguin. ISBN 0-670-87144-3.

Brown, D. Anne. 1995. *You Can Get There from Here: Life Lessons on Growth and Self Discovery for the Black Woman.* Bryant & Dillon Publishers. ISBN 0-9638672-6-1.

Brown, Dennis, and Pamela Toussaint. 1998. *Mama's Little Baby: The Black Woman's Guide to Pregnancy, Childbirth and Baby's First Year.* Dutton/Plume. ISBN 0-4522741-9-2.

Brown, Les. 1998. *It's Not Over until You Win: How to Become the Person You Always Wanted to Be—No Matter What the Obstacle.* Simon & Schuster. ISBN 0-6848352-8-2.

Brown, Lloyd L. 1996. *The Young Paul Robeson: On My Journey Now.* Westview Press. ISBN 0-8133317-8-1.

Brown, Sterling A. 1996. *A Son's Return: Selected Essays of Sterling A. Brown.* Edited by Mark A. Sanders. Northeastern University Press. ISBN 1-55553-275-6.

Brown, Tony. 1997. *Black Lies, White Lies: The Truth according to Tony Brown.* HarperTrade. ISBN 0-6881513-1-0.

———. 1998. *Empower the People: A 7-Step Plan to Overthrow the Conspiracy That Is Stealing Your Money and Freedom.* William Morrow. ISBN 0-6881576-2-9.

Brown, Tracey L. 1998. *The Life and Times of Ron Brown.* Morrow/Avon. ISBN 0-6881532-0-8.

Broyard, Anatole. 1997. *Kafka Was the Rage: A Greenwich Village Memoir.* Vintage Books. ISBN 0-6797812-6-9.

Bryant, Thelma Harper. 1996. *The Memoirs of the Harper Family (1865–1995).* Vantage Press. ISBN 0-5331196-6-9.

Bunkley, Crawford B. 1996. *The African-American Network: Get Connected to more than 5,000 Prominent People and Organizations in the African-American Community.* Dutton/Plume. ISBN 0-4522749-3-1.

Burns, Ben. 1996. *Nitty Gritty: A White Editor in Black Journalism.* University of Mississippi. ISBN 0-87805-812-.

Burris, John L., with Catherine Whitney. 1999. *Blue vs. Black: Blacks and Cops in Conflict and What We Can Do about It.* St. Martin's Press. ISBN 0-312-20392-6.

Bush, Roderick D. 2000. *We Are Not What We Seem: Black Nationalism and Class Struggle in the American Century.* New York University Press. ISBN 0-8147131-8-1.

Cadet, Jean-Robert. 1998. *Restavec: From Haitian Slave Child to Middle-Class American.* University of Texas Press. ISBN 0-2927120-3-0.

Caldwell, Earl. 1994. *Black American Witness: Reports from the Front.* Lion House Publishers. ISBN 1-88-6446-10-5.

Campbell, Bebe Moore. 1999. *Singing in the Comeback Choir.* Berkley Publishing Group. ISBN 0-4251666-2-7.

Campbell, Clarice T. 1997. *Civil Rights Chronicle: Letters from the South.* University Press of Mississippi. ISBN 0-8780595-2-0.

Canada, Geoffrey. 1998. *Reaching Up for Manhood: Transforming the Lives of Boys in America.* Beacon Press. ISBN 0-8070231-6-7.

Cannon, Katie G. 1995. *Katie's Canon: Womanism and the Soul of the Black Community.* Continuum. ISBN 0-8264-0834-6.

Cannon, Lou. 1999. *Official Negligence: How Rodney King and the Riots Changed Los Angeles and the LAPD.* Westview Press. ISBN 0-8133372-5-9.

Capeci, Jr., Dominic. 1998. *The Lynching of Cleo Wright.* University of Kentucky Press. ISBN 0-8131-2048-9.

Caplan, Marvin. 1999. *Farther Along: A Civil Rights Memoir.* Louisiana State University Press. ISBN 0-8071235-2-8.

Carbado, Devon. 1999. *Black Men on Race, Gender and Sexuality: A Critical Reader.* New York University Press. ISBN 0-8147155-3-2.

Caretta, Vincent, ed. 1996. *Unchained Voices: An Anthology of Black Authors in the English-Speaking World of the Eighteenth Century.* University Press of Kentucky. ISBN 0-8131088-4-5.

Carroll, Rebecca. 1997. *Sugar in the Raw: Voices of Young Black Girls in America.* Random House. ISBN 0-5178849-7-6.

Carruthers, Jacob. 1997. *Intellectual Warfare.* Third World Press. ISBN 0-88378-160-3.

Carter, Dan T. 1996. *From George Wallace to Newt Gingrich: Race in the Conservative Counterrevolution 1963-1994.* Louisiana State University Press. ISBN 0-8071-2118-5.

Carter, Stephen L. 1991. *Reflections of an Affirmative Action Baby.* Basic Books. ISBN 0-465-06871-5.

————. 1997. *Integrity.* HarperTrade. ISBN 0-0609280-7-7.

————. 1998. *Civility: Manners, Morals and the Etiquette of Democracy.* Basic Books. ISBN 0-4650238-4-3.

Cassuto, Leonard. 1996. *The Inhuman Race: The Racial Grotesque in American Literature and Culture.* Columbia University Press. ISBN 0-2311033-7-9.

Century, Douglas. 1999. *Street Kingdom: Five Years inside the Franklin Avenue Posse.* Warner Books. ISBN 0-4465226-6-x.

Chadwick, Bruce. 1997. *When the Game Was Black and White: The Illustrated History of Baseball's Negro Leagues.* Abbeville. ISBN 0-89660-091-2.

Chambers, Jack. 1998. *Milestones: The Music and Times of Miles Davis.* Da Capo Press. ISBN 0-3068084-9-8.

Chekwas, Dr. Sam. 1998. *The 100 Steps Necessary for Survival in America for People of Color.* Seaburn Books. ISBN 1-8857784-7-3.

Chideya, Farai. 1999. *The Color of Our Future: Our Multi-Racial Future.* Morrow. ISBN 0-6881653-0-3.

Chireau, Yvonne, and Nathaniel Deutsch, eds. 1999. *Black Zion: African American Religious Encounters with Judaism.* Oxford University Press. ISBN 0-1951125-7-1.

Chuck D., with Yusuf Jah. 1997. *Fight the Power: Rap, Race and Reality.* Foreword by Spike Lee. Delacorte. ISBN 0-385-31868-5.

Cimbala, Paul A., and Robert F. Himmelberg. 1996. *Historians and Race: Autobiography and the Writing of History.* Indiana University Press. ISBN 0-2533323-5-4.

Clarke, Donald. 1995. *Wishing on the Moon: The Life and Times of Billie Holiday.* Penguin. ISBN 0-1402475-4-8.

Clarke, John Henrik. 1997. *My Life in Search of Africa.* Third World Press. ISBN 0-88378-158-1.

————, ed. 1997. *The Second Crucifixion of Nat Turner.* Black Classic Press. ISBN 0-933121-95-4.

Clegg, Claude A. 1999. *An Original Man: The Life and Times of Elijah Muhammad.* St. Martin's Press. ISBN 0-3122073-5-2.

Clinton, Catherine, and Michele Gillespie, eds. 1997. *The Devil's Lane: Sex and Race in the Early South.* Oxford University Press. ISBN 0-19-511243-1.

Cochran, David Carroll. 1999. *The Color of Freedom: Race and Contemporary American Liberalism.* State University of New York Press. ISBN 0-7914418-6-5.

Cochran, Jr., Johnnie L., with Tim Rutten. 1996. *Journey to Justice.* One World, Ballantine. ISBN 0-345-40583-8.

Coen, Cathy J. 1999. *The Boundaries of Blackness: AIDS and the Breakdown of Black Politics.* University of Chicago Press. ISBN 0-226-11289-6.

Cohadas, Nadine. 1997. *The Band Played Dixie: Race and the Liberal Conscience at Ole Miss.* Free Press. ISBN 0-684-82721-2.

Cole, David. 1999. *No Equal Justice: Race and Class in the American Criminal Justice System.* New Press. ISBN 1-56584-473-4.

Coleman, Christena. 1997. *Mama Knows Best: African-American Wives Tales, Myths, and Remedies for Mothers and Mothers-to-Be.* Simon & Schuster. ISBN 0-6848342-6-x.

Coleman, Jonathan. 1997. *Long Way to Go: Black and White in America.* Atlantic Monthly Press. ISBN 0-87113-692-9.

Collier, Peter, and David Horowitz, eds. 1997. *The Race Card: White Guilt, Black Resentment, and the Assault on Truth and Justice.* Prima/Forum. ISBN 0-7615-0942-9.

Collins, David R. 1994. *Arthur Ashe: Against the Wind.* Silver Burdett Ginn. ISBN 0-87518-647-5.

Collins, Marva. 1996. *Values: Lighting the Candle of Excellence. A Practical Guide for the Family.* New Star Media. ISBN 0-7871104-0-x.

Collins, Sharon M. 1996. *Black Corporate Executives: The Making and Breaking of a Black Middle Class.* Temple University Press. ISBN 1-5663947-3-2.

Collison, Gary L. 1998. *Shadrach Minkins: From Fugitive Slave to Citizen.* Harvard University Press. ISBN 0-6748029-9-3.

Colwell, Robert E. 1996. *Love Leaves No Regrets: An Insightful View of Displaced Children through the Eyes of a Former Foster Child.* Duncan & Duncan Publishers. ISBN 1878647-28-8.

Cone, James H. 2000. *Risks of Faith: The Emergence of a Black Theology of Liberation, 1968–1998.* Beacon Press. ISBN 0-8070095-1-2.

Conway, Jill Ker. 1998. *When Memory Speaks: Reflections on Autobiography.* Knopf. ISBN 0-6794459-3-5.

Cool, L. L., and Karen Hunter. 1997. *I Make My Own Rules.* St. Martin's Press. ISBN 0-3121711-0-2.

Cornish, Grace. 1998. *10 Bad Choices that Ruin Black Women's Lives.* Crown. ISBN 0-6096005-0-8.

Cose, Ellis. 1997. *Color-Blind: Seeing beyond Race in a Race-Obsessed World.* HarperCollins. ISBN 0-06-017497-8.

————, ed. 1997. *The Darden Dilemma.* HarperTrade. ISBN 0-0609522-7-x.

Cottman, Michael H. 1998. *The Wreck of the Henrietta Marie: An African-American's Spiritual Journey to Uncover a Sunken Slave Ship's Past.* Harmony. ISBN 0-517-70328-9.

Coutinho, Joao D. 1998. *A Kind of Absence: Life in the Shadow of History.* Yuganta Press. ISBN 0-9389991-0-9.

Crawford, Colin. 1996. *Uproar at Dancing Rabbit Creek: The Battle over Race, Class, and the Environment in the New South.* Addison-Wesley. ISBN 0-2016272-3-x.

Crawford, Vicki L., et al., eds. 1993. *Women in the Civil Rights Movement: Trailblazers and Torchbearers, 1941–1965.* Indiana University Press. ISBN 0-2532083-2-7.

Crouch, Stanley. 1997. *The All-American Skin Game: Or, The Decoy of Race.* Random House. ISBN 0-6797766-0-5.

————. 1998. *Always in Pursuit: Fresh American Perspectives, 1995–1997.* Pantheon. ISBN 0-375-40153-9.

Cruse, Harold. 1984. *The Crisis of the Negro Intellectual: An Analysis of the Failure of Black Leadership.* HarperTrade. ISBN 0-688-03886-7.

Cugoano, Ottobah, Vincent Carretta, et al. 1999. *Thoughts and Sentiments on the Evils of Slavery and Other Writings.* Penguin USA. ISBN 0-1404475-0-4.

Cummings, Terrance. 1996. *Too Hot to Cool Down.* Stewart Tabori & Chang. ISBN 1-5567051-0-7.

Curriden, Mark, and Leroy Phillips, Jr. 2001. *Contempt of Court: The Turn-of-the-Century Lynching That Launched a Hundred Years of Federalism.* Vintage Anchor Publishing. ISBN 0-3857208-2-3.

Curry, Constance. 1999. *Silver Rights.* Algonquin Books of Chapel Hill. ISBN 1-5651209-5-7.

Curry, George E. 1996. *The Affirmative Action Debate.* Addison-Wesley. ISBN 0-2014796-3-X.

Curtis, Susan. 1998. *The First Black Actors on the Great White Way.* University of Missouri Press. ISBN 0-8262-1195-X.

D'Aguiar, Fred. 1999. *Feeding the Ghosts.* Ecco Press. ISBN 0-8800162-3-X.

Dahl, Linda. 2000. *Morning Glory: A Biography of Mary Lou Williams.* Pantheon. ISBN 0-3754089-9-1.

Dalton, Harlon L. 1996. *Racial Healing: Confronting the Fear between Blacks and Whites.* Doubleday. ISBN 0-3854751-7-9.

Dance, Daryl Cumber, ed. 1997. *Honey, Hush!: An Anthology of African American Women's Humor.* Norton. ISBN 0-393-04557-9.

Danchin, Sebastian. 1998. *'Blues Boy': The Life and Music of B. B. King.* University Press of Mississippi. ISBN 1-5780601-7-6.

Daniels, Pearl Gray. 1997. *The History of the Holt Street Church of Christ and Its Role in Establishing Churches of Christ among African Americans in Central Alabama 1928–1997.* American Literary Press. ISBN 1-56167-385-4.

Daniels, Roger. 1997. *Not Like Us: Immigrants and Minorities in America, 1890–1924.* Ivan R. Dee. ISBN 1-56663-165-3.

Danquah, Meeri Nana. 2001. *Becoming American: Personal Essays by First Generation Immigrant Women.* Hyperion. ISBN 0-7868834-3-x.

Danquah, Meri Nana-Ama. 1999. *Willow Weep for Me: A Black Woman's Journey through Depression.* Ballantine Publishing Group. ISBN 0-3454321-3-4.

Darden, Christopher, with Jess Walter. 1996. *In Contempt.* Harper-Trade. ISBN 0-06-039183-9.

Dash, Leon. 1996. *Rosa Lee: A Mother and Her Family in Urban America.* Basic Books. ISBN 0-465-07092-2.

Dash, Michael I. N., Jonathan Jackson, et al. 1997. *Hidden Wholeness: An African American Spirituality for Individuals and Communities.* Pilgrim Press. ISBN 0-82981164-8.

Daughtry, Herbert D. 1997. *No Monopoly on Suffering.* Africa World Press. ISBN 0-8654358-6-3.

Davis, Angela Y. 1998. *The Angela Y. Davis Reader.* Edited by Joy James. Blackwell Publishers. ISBN 0-631-0360-5.

———. 1998. *Blues Legacies and Black Feminism.* Pantheon. ISBN 0-6794500-5-x.

Davis, Daryl. 1998. *Klan-Destine Relationships: A Black Man's Odyssey in the Ku Klux Klan.* New Horizon. ISBN 0-88282-159-8.

Davis, Eric. 1999. *Born to Play: The Eric Davis Story: Life Lessons in Overcoming Adversity on and off the Field.* Viking. ISBN 0-670-88511-8.

Davis, George. 1998. *Love Lessons: African Americans and Sex, Romance and Marriage in the Nineties.* Morrow. ISBN 0-688-14864-6.

Davis, Ossie, and Ruby Dee. 2000. *With Ossie and Ruby: In This Life Together.* Morrow/Avon. ISBN 0-6881758-2-1.

Davis, Terrell. 1998. *TD: Dreams in Motion.* HarperCollins. ISBN 0-0601928-2-8.

Davis, Townsend. 1999. *Weary Feet, Rested Souls: A Guided History through the Civil Rights Movement.* Norton. ISBN 0-3933181-9-2.

Davis, Tracey, with Dolores Barclay. 1996. *Sammy Davis Jr., My Father.* General Publishing. ISBN 1-881649-84-9.

Davis-Adeshote, Jeannette. 1995. *Black Survival in White America: From Past History to the Next Century.* Bryant & Dillon Publishers. ISBN 0-9638672-3-7.

de Wilde, Laurent. 1998. *Monk.* Marlowe & Company. ISBN 1-56924-740-4.

Deats, Richard. 1999. *Martin Luther King, Jr., Spirit-Led Prophet: A Biography.* New City Press. ISBN 1-5654809-7-x.

DeCaro, Jr., Louis A. 1995. *On the Side of My People: A Religious Life of Malcolm X.* New York University Press. ISBN 0-8147-1864-7.

Delany, Sarah L., with Amy Hill Hearth. 1996. *On My Own at 107: Reflections on Life without Bessie.* Harper San Francisco. ISBN 0-06-251485-7.

DeMott, Benjamin. 1998. *The Trouble with Friendship. Why Americans Can't Think Straight about Race.* Yale University Press. ISBN 0-3000739-4-1.

Dent, David J. 2001. *In Search of Black America: Discovering the African-American Dream.* Simon & Schuster. ISBN 0-7432030-5-4.

Dent, Tom. 1997. *Southern Journey: My Return to the Civil Rights Movement.* Morrow. ISBN 0-6881409-9-8.

Derricotte, Toi. 1999. *The Black Notebooks: An Interior Journey.* Norton. ISBN 0-3933190-1-6.

Dickerson, Dennis C. 1998. *Militant Mediator: Whitney M. Young, Jr.* University Press of Kentucky. ISBN 0-8131-2058-6.

Diedrich, Maria. 1999. *Love across Color Lines: Ottillie Assing and Frederick Douglass.* Hill & Wang. ISBN 0-8090161-3-3.

Dinesen, Isak. 1993. *Out of Africa.* Bucaneer Books. ISBN 089968440.

Dobson, Shireen, and Teresa Barker. 1997. *The Mother-Daughter Book Club.* HarperCollins. ISBN 0-0609524-2-3.

Douglas, Kelly Brown. 1999. *Sexuality and the Black Church: A Womanist Perspective.* Orbis Books. ISBN 1-5707524-2-7.

Downs, Donald A. 1999. *Cornell '69: Liberalism and the Crisis of the American University.* Cornell University Press. ISBN 0-8014365-3-2.

Dryden, Charles W. 1997. *A-Train: Memoir of a Tuskegee Airman.* University of Alabama Press. ISBN 0-8173085-6-3.

D'Souza, Dinesh. 1996. *The End of Racism: Principles for a Multiracial Society.* Simon & Schuster. ISBN 0-6848252-4-4.

Du Bois, W. E. B. 1903. *The Souls of Black Folk.* A.C. McClurg & Co.

duCille, Anne. 1996. *Skin Trade.* Harvard University Press. ISBN 0-674-81084-8.

Dunbar, Harry B. 1995. *A Brother Like Me: A Memoir.* Queenhyte. ISBN 0-9643654-0-5.

Dunn, Marvin. 1997. *Black Miami in the Twentieth Century.* University Press of Florida. ISBN 0-8130153-0-8.

Dyson, Michael Eric. 1996. *Between God and Gangsta Rap. Bearing Witness to Black Culture.* Oxford University Press. ISBN 0-1950989-8-6.

Dyson, Michael Eric. 1997. *Race Rules: Navigating the Color Line.* Vintage Books. ISBN 0-6797815-6-0.

———. 2000. *Making Malcolm: The Myth and Meaning of Malcolm X.* Replica Books. ISBN 0-7351026-1-9.

———. 2001. *I May Not Get There with You: The True Martin Luther King Jr.* Simon & Schuster. ISBN 0-6848303-7-x.

Early, Gerald, ed. 1998. *Ain't but a Place: An Anthology of African American Writings about St. Louis.* University of Missouri Press. ISBN 1-883982-27-8.

———, ed. 1998. *The Muhammad Ali Reader.* HarperCollins. ISBN 0-88001-602-7.

Eastland, Terry. 1999. *Ending Affirmative Action.* Basic Books. ISBN 0-6141596-5-5.

Edelman, Marian Wright. 2000. *Lanterns: A Memoir of Mentors.* HarperTrade. ISBN 0-0609585-9-6.

Edley, Jr., Christopher. 1996. *Not All Black and White: Affirmative Action, Race, and American Values.* Hill & Wang. ISBN 0-8090-2955-3.

Edwards, Jr., Jefferson. 1996. *Purging Racism from Christianity: Freedom and Purpose through Identity.* Zondervan Publishing. ISBN 0-3102019-5-0.

Egerton, John. 1995. *Speak Now against the Day: The Generation before the Civil Rights Movement in the South.* Chapel Hill Books, University of North Carolina. ISBN 0-8078455-7-4.

Ehrhart-Morrison, Dorothy. 1997. *No Mountain High Enough: Secrets of Successful African-American Women.* Conari Press. ISBN 0-9432339-8-4.

Ehui, Felix. 1998. *What If Blacks Did Not Exist?* African American Images. ISBN 0-9135435-6-x.

Eklof, Barbara J. 1997. *For Every Season.* HarperCollins. ISBN 0-0601781-8-3.

Elders, Jocelyn, and David Chanoff. 1997. *Jocelyn Elders, M.D.: From Sharecropper's Daughter to Surgeon General of the United States.* Thorndike Press. ISBN 0-7862095-8-5.

Eldon, Kathy, ed. 1997. *The Journey Is the Destination: The Journals of Dan Eldon.* Chronicle Books. ISBN 0-8118158-6-2.

Elliott, Max. 1997. *Ms. Thang: Real Knights Don't Show Up at 3 in the Morning: What Every Black Woman Needs to Know about Love, Intimacy, and Relationships.* Pocket Books. ISBN 0-671-00235-x.

Ellison, Ralph. 1995. *The Collected Essays of Ralph Ellison.* Edited by John F. Callahan. Random House. ISBN 0-6796017-6-7.

————. 1995. *Shadow and Act.* Vintage Books. ISBN 067976008.

Emeka, Mauris. 1994. *AMTRAKing.* Apollo Publishing Company. ISBN 0-9640125-0-2.

Entine, Jon. n.d. *Taboo: Why Black Athletes Dominate Sports and Why We're Afraid to Talk about It.* Public Affairs. ISBN 1-5864802-6-x.

Entman, Robert M., and Andrew Rojecki. 2000. *The Black Image in the White Mind.* University of Chicago Press. ISBN 0-2262107-5-8.

Epstein, Daniel Mark. 2000. *Nat King Cole.* Northeastern University Press. ISBN 1-5555346-9-4.

Eskew, Glenn T. 1997. *But for Birmingham: The Local and National Movements in the Civil Rights Struggle.* University of North Carolina Press. ISBN 0-8078-2363-5.

Estwick, Randolph R. 2000. *Successful Journey: Not without Pain.* Vantage Press. ISBN 0-533-13289-4.

Evers, Charles, and Andrew Szanton. 1996. *Have No Fear: The Charles Evers Story.* John Wiley. ISBN 0-471-12251-3.

Evers-Williams, Myrlie. 1999. *Watch Me Fly: What I learned on the Way to Becoming the Woman I Was Meant to Be.* Little Brown. ISBN 0-316-25520-3.

Faber, Eli. 1998. *Jews, Slaves and the Slave Trade: Setting The Record Straight.* New York University Press. ISBN 0-8147263-8-0.

Fair, Bryan K. 1999. *Notes of a Racial Caste Baby: Colorblindness and the End of Affirmative Action.* New York University Press. ISBN 0-8147265-2-6.

Fairclough, Adam. 1995. *Race and Democracy: The Civil Rights Struggle in Louisiana, 1915–1972.* University of Georgia Press. ISBN 0-8203170-0-4.

Faryna, Stan, Brad Stetson, and Joseph Conti, eds. 1997. *Black and Right: The Bold New Voice of Black Conservatives in America.* Greenwood Publishing Group. ISBN 0-275-95342-4.

Feagin, Joe R., Hernan Vera, and N. O. Imani. 1996. *The Agony of Education: Black Students at a White University.* Routledge. ISBN 0-415-91511-2.

Feinstein, John. 1998. *The First Coming: Tiger Woods: Master or Martyr?* Ballantine Publishing Group. ISBN 0-345-42286-4.

Fernandez, John. 1998. *Race and Rhetoric: The True State of Race and Gender Relations in Corporate America.* McGraw-Hill. ISBN 0-07-022008-5.

Fetzer, Philip L., ed. 1996. *The Ethnic Moment: The Search for Equality in the American Experience.* M.E. Sharpe. ISBN 1-56324-926-x.

Fischer, Perry, and Brooks Gray. 1994. *Blacks and Whites Together through Hell: U.S. Marines in World War II.* Millsmont Publishers. ISBN 0-9623257-1-6.

Flake, Floyd, and Donna M. Williams. 1999. *The Way of the Boot-strapper: Nine Action Steps for Achieving Your Dreams.* Harper San Francisco. ISBN 0-06-251595-0.

Flax, Jane. 1998. *The American Dream in Black and White: The Clarence Thomas Hearings.* Cornell University Press. ISBN 0-8014-3575-7.

Fleming, Robert. 2000. *The African American Writers Handbook: How to Get in Print and Stay in Print.* Ballantine Publishing Group. ISBN 0-3454232-7-5.

Fleming, Thomas C. n.d. *Reflections on Black History*. Part 1: *Jacksonville and Harlem, 1907–1919*. Max Millard. ISBN 0-9962887-0-x.

Flipper, Henry Ossian. 1998. *The Colored Cadet at West Point: Autobiography of Lieut. Henry Ossian Flipper, U.S.A., First Graduate of Color from the U.S. Military Academy*. Introduction by Quintard Taylor, Jr. University of Nebraska Press. ISBN 0-8032-6890-4.

Foner, Philip Sheldon. 1998. *Lift Every Voice: African American Oratory, 1787–1900*. University of Alabama Press. ISBN 0-8173084-8-2.

Foreman, George, and Joel Engel. 1995. *By George: The Autobiography of George Foreman*. Villard. ISBN 0-6794439-4-0.

Foster, Michele. 1998. *Black Teachers on Teaching*. New Press. ISBN 1-5658445-3-x.

Fountain, Joan. 1998. *Nothing Bad Happens, Ever*. Warner Books. ISBN 0-4465234-1-0.

Frady, Marshall. 1998. *Jesse: The Life and Pilgrimage of Jesse Jackson*. Random House. ISBN 0-5173118-7-9.

Fraim, John. 1996. *Spirit Catcher: The life and Art of John Coltrane*. Greathouse Company. ISBN 0-9645561-0-3.

Frank, Linnie, and Andria Hall. 1998. *This Far by Faith: How to Put God First in Everyday Living*. Doubleday. ISBN 0-3854926-0-x.

Frankel, Noralee. 1999. *Freedom's Women: Black Women and Families in Civil War Era Mississippi*. Indiana University Press. ISBN 0-2533349-5-0.

Franklin, John Hope, and John Whittington Franklin. 2000. *My Life and an Era: The Autobiography of Buck Colbert Franklin*. Louisiana State University Press. ISBN 0-8071259-9-7.

Franklin, John Hope, and Loren Schweninger. 2000. *Runaway Slaves: Rebel on the Plantation, 1790–1860*. Oxford University Press. ISBN 0-1950845-1-9.

Franklin, Robert M. 1997. *Another Day's Journey: Black Churches Confronting the American Crisis.* Augsburg Fortress Publishers. ISBN 0-8006309-6-3.

Franks, Gary. 1996. *Searching for the Promised Land: An African-American's Optimistic Odyssey.* HarperCollins. ISBN 0-06-039156-1.

Fraser, George. 1999. *Race for Success: The Ten Best Business Opportunities for Blacks in America.* Morrow/Avon. ISBN 0-3807298-9-x.

Frazier, E. Franklin. 1997. *Black Bourgeoisie.* Free Press. ISBN 0-6848324-1-0.

Fredrickson, George M. 1996. *Black Liberation. A Comparative History of Black Ideologies in the United States and South Africa.* Oxford University Press. ISBN 0-1951097-8-3.

Freedman, Estelle B. 1989. *Intimate Matters: A History of Sensuality in America.* Harper & Row. ISBN 0-0609155-0-1.

Fremon, David K. 1994. *The Negro Baseball Leagues.* Silver Burdett Ginn. ISBN 0-02-735695-7.

Fuller, Ameenah. 1996. *Stop the Black Man Now!* Looking-In Publications. ISBN 0-9653614-0-3.

Fulwood III, Sam. 1996. *Waking from the Dream: My Life in the Black Middle Class.* Doubleday. ISBN 0-3854782 2 4.

Funderburg, Lise. 1994. *Black, White, Other: Biracial Americans Talk about Race and Identity.* Morrow/Avon. ISBN 0-6881182-4-0.

Gaines, Patrice. 1996. *Laughing in the Dark: From Colored Girl to Woman of Color—A Journey from Prison to Power.* African American Images. ISBN 0-6142233-0-x.

————. 1997. *Moments of Grace: Meeting the Challenge to Change.* Crown. ISBN 0-5177043-3-1.

Gallen, David, ed. 1995. *Malcolm X: As They Knew Him.* One World, Ballantine. ISBN 0-3454005-2-6.

Gardell, Mattias. 1996. *In the Name of Elijah Muhammad: Louis Farrakhan and the Nation of Islam.* Duke University Press. ISBN 0-8223-1845-8.

Gardner, James. 1997. *The Age of Extremism: The End of Compromise in American Politics, Culture and Race Relations.* Carol Publishing/Birch Lane. ISBN 1-5597238-8-2.

Garrod, Andrew, et al., eds. 1999. *Souls Looking Back: Portraits of Growing Up Black.* Routledge. ISBN 0-415-92062-0.

Gaspar, David B, and Darlene Clark Hine, eds. 1996. *More Than Chattel: Black Women and Slavery in the Americas.* Indiana University Press. ISBN 0-2533301-7-3.

Gates, Jr., Henry Louis. 1994. *Colored People: A Memoir.* Alfred A. Knopf. ISBN 0-679-42179-3.

————. 1997. *The Slave Narrative of Frederick Douglass.* Dell. ISBN 0-4402222-8-1.

————. 1997. *Thirteen Ways of Looking at a Black Man.* Random House. ISBN 0-679-45713-5.

Gates, Jr., Henry Louis, and Nellie Y. McKay. 1996. *The Norton Anthology of African-American Literature.* Norton. ISBN 0-3939590-8-2.

Gates, Jr., Henry Louis, and Cornel West. 1997. *The Future of the Race.* Vintage Books. ISBN 067976383.

Gatlin, June. 1995. *The Spirit Speaks to Sisters: Inspiration and Empowerment for Black Women.* Noble Press. ISBN 1-879360-39-x.

Gerzina, Gretchen. 1997. *Black London.* Rutgers University Press. ISBN 0-8135225-9-5.

Gibbs, Jewelle T. 1996. *Race and Justice in America: Rodney King and O. J. Simpson in a House Divided.* Jossey-Bass. ISBN 0-7879026-4-0.

Gibbs, Mifflin Wistar. 1995. *Mifflin Wistar Gibbs: Shadow and Light: An Autobioraphy.* Introduction by Booker T. Washington and Tom W. Dillard. University of Nebraska Press. ISBN 0-8032705-0-x.

Giddings, Joshua R. 1997. *The Exiles of Florida.* Black Classic Press. ISBN 0-933121-47-4.

Gilbert, Olive. 1997. *The Narrative of Sojourner Truth.* Dover Publications. ISBN 0-4862989-9-x.

Gilligan, Carol, and Amy Sullivan. 1995. *Between Voice and Silence: Women and Girls, Race and Relationships.* Harvard University Press. ISBN 0-674-06879-3.

Gilmore, Glenda Elizabeth. 1996. *Gender and Jim Crow: Women and the Politics of White Supremacy in North Carolina, 1895–1920.* University of North Carolina Press. ISBN 0-8078-4596-5.

Givens, Archie, ed. 1997. *Spirited Minds: African American Books for Our Sons and Our Brothers.* Norton. ISBN 0-3933173-9-0.

Gladwell, Malcolm. 2000. *The Tipping Point: How Little Things Can Make a Big Difference.* Little Brown. ISBN 0-3163169-6-2.

Glazer, Nathan. 1998. *We Are All Multiculturalsts Now.* Harvard University Press. ISBN 0-6749483-6-x.

Goldberg, Whoopi. 1998. *Book.* Morrow/Avon. ISBN 0-3807297-9-2.

Goldfield, Michael. 1997. *The Color of Politics: Race, Class, and The Mainsprings of American Politics.* New Press. ISBN 1-565854-325-8.

Gomes, Peter J. 1999. *The Good Book: Reading the Bible with Mind and Heart.* Avon Books. ISBN 0-380-72323-9.

Gomez-Jefferson, Ann. 1998. *In Darkness with God: The Life of Joseph Gomez, a Bishop in the African Methodist Episcopal Church.* Kent State University Press. ISBN 0-8733860-7-8.

Gordon, Edmund W. 1999. *Education and Justice: A View from the Back of the Bus.* Teachers College Press. ISBN 0-8077-3844-1.

Gordon, Jacob, and Elmer Jackson, Jr. n.d. *The History of the National Bar Association.* Third World Press. ISBN 0-88378-186-7.

Gordon, Vivian Verdell. 1987. *Black Women, Feminism, and Black Liberation.* Third World Press. ISBN 0-88378-111-5.

Gordon-Reed, Annette. 1998. *Thomas Jefferson and Sally Hemings: An American Controversy.* University Press of Virginia. ISBN 0-8139183-3-2.

Gourse, Leslie. 1997. *Billie Holiday Companion: Seven Decades of Commentary.* Music Sales Corporation. ISBN 0-0286461-3-4.

———. 1999. *Wynton Marsalis: Skain's Domain, a Biography.* Schirmer. ISBN 0-02-864863-3.

———. n.d. *The Ella Fitzgerald Companion: Six Decades of Commentary.* Music Sales Corporation. ISBN 0-0286462-5-8.

———. n.d. *Straight, No Chaser: The Life and Genius of Thelonius Monk.* Music Sales Corporation. ISBN 0-8256722-9-5.

Govenar, Alan B., and Jay F. Brakefield. 1998. *Deep Ellum and Central Track: Where the Black and White Worlds of Dallas Converged.* University of North Texas Press. ISBN 1-57441-051-2.

Graetz, Robert S. 1999. *A White Preacher's Memoir: The Montgomery Bus Boycott.* Black Belt. ISBN 1-57966-015-0.

Graham, Lawrence O. 1999. *Our Kind of People: Inside America's Black Upper Class.* HarperCollins. ISBN 0-06-018352-7.

Graham, Stedman. 1998. *You Can Make It Happen.* Simon & Schuster. ISBN 064843226.

Grant, Joanne. 1999. *Ella Baker: Freedom Bound.* John Wiley. ISBN 0-4713271-7-4.

Gravely, II, Melvin J. 1995. *The Black Entrepreneur's Guide to Success.* Duncan & Duncan Publishers. ISBN 1-878647-20-2.

Graves, Earl G. 1998. *How to Succeed in Business without Being White: Success Strategies from America's Premiere Black Entrepreneur.* HarperCollins. ISBN 0-8873090-9-7.

Gray, Herman. 1997. *Watching Race: Television and the Struggle for "Blackness."* University of Minnesota Press. ISBN 0-8166225-1-5.

Green, Carl R. 1994. *Jackie Joyner-Kersee.* Silver Burdett Ginn. ISBN 0-89686-838-9.

Greenberg, Alan. 1994. *Love in Vain: A Vision of Robert Johnson.* Oxford University Press. ISBN 0-3068055-7-X.

Griffin, John Howard. 1999. *Black Like Me.* Dutton/Plume. ISBN 0-4522776-6-3.

Griffin, Paul R. 1999. *Seeds of Racism in the Soul of America.* Pilgrim Press/United Church Press. ISBN 0-8298131-3-6.

Griffith, Ezra E. H. 1998. *Race and Excellent: My Dialogue with Chester Pierce.* University of Iowa Press. ISBN 0-87745-628-3.

Gubar, Susan. 2000. *Racechanges: White Skin, Black Face in American Culture.* Oxford University Press. ISBN 0-1951341-8-4.

Guerrero, Ed. 1993. *Framing Blackness: The African American Image in Film.* Temple University Press. ISBN 1-5663912-5-3.

Guillory, Monique, and Richard C. Green, eds. 1997. *Soul: Black Power, Politics, and Pleasure.* New York University Press. ISBN 0-8147308-4-1.

Guinier, Lani. 1998. *Lift Every Voice: Turning a Civil Rights Setback into a New Vision of Social Justice.* Simon & Schuster. ISBN 0-684-81145-6.

Guinier, Lani, Michelle Fine, and Jane Balin. 1998. *Becoming Gentlemen: Women, Law School, and Institutional Change.* Beacon Press. ISBN 0-8070440-5-9.

Haizlip, Shirlee Taylor, and Harold C. Haizlip. 1998. *In the Garden of Our Dreams: Memoirs of a Marriage.* Kodansha America. ISBN 1-56836-254-4.

Hajdu, David. 1996. *Lush Life: A Biography of Billy Strayhorn.* Farrar, Straus & Giroux. ISBN 0-3741943-8-6.

Halberstam, David. 1998. *The Children.* Random House. ISBN0-6794156-1-0.

Hale, Jr., Frank W. 1996. *Angels Watching over Me: The Autobiography of Dr. Frank W. Hale Jr.* Winston-Derek. ISBN 1-5552378-1-9.

Hall, Gwendolyn Midlo. 1995. *Love, War, and the 96th Engineers (Colored): The World War II New Guinea Diaries of Captain Hyman Samuelson.* University of Illinois Press. ISBN 0-2520217-9-7.

Hall, Wade. 1997. *Passing for Black: The Life and Careers of Mae Street Kidd.* University Press of Kentucky. ISBN 0-8131-0948-5.

Halliburton, Warren J. 1970. *America's Majorities and Minorities.* Ayer Company Publishers. ISBN 0-4050028-2-3.

————. 1972. *Harlem, a History of Broken Dreams.* Doubleday. ISBN 0-3850584-0-3.

————. [1972] 1984. *The Picture Life of Michael Jackson.* Franklin Watts. ISBN 0-5310487-9-9.

————. 1978. *Fighting Red Tails: America's First Black Airmen.* Silver Burdett Ginn. ISBN 0-8954706-1-6.

————. 1992. *African Wildlife.* Macmillan. ISBN 0-8968667-4-2.

————. 1992. *Africa's Struggle for Independence.* Silver Burdett Ginn. ISBN 0-8968667-9-3.

————. 1993. *African Industries.* Silver Burdett Ginn. ISBN 0-8968667-2-6.

————. 1993. *African Landscapes.* Silver Burdett Ginn. ISBN 0-8968667-3-4.

————. 1993. *Clarence Thomas: Supreme Court Justice.* Enslow Publishers. ISBN 0-8949041-4-0.

————. 1993. *Historic Speeches of African Americans.* Franklin Watts. ISBN 0-5311103-4-6.

————. 1994. *Coming to America: The West Indian–American Experience.* Millbrook Press. ISBN 1-56294-340-5.

————. n.d. *America's Color Caravan.* Singer-Graflex.

Halliburton, Warren J., Eric Broudy, and Laurence Swinburne. n.d. *They Had a Dream.* Pyramid Books.

Halliburton, Warren J., and Susan Grossman, eds. 1993. *City and Village Life.* Silver Burdett Ginn. ISBN 0-8968667-7-7.

Halliburton, Warren J., and William Loren Katz. n.d. *A History of Black Americans.* Harcourt Brace.

Halliburton, Warren J., and Kathilyn Probosz, eds. 1992. *Nomads of the Sahara.* Maxwell Macmillan International. ISBN 0-8968667-8-5.

————, eds. 1993. *Africa's Struggle to Survive.* Silver Burdett Ginn. ISBN 0-8968667-5-0.

Halsell, Grace. 1996. *In Their Shoes: A White Woman's Journey Living as a Black, Navajo and Mexical Illegal.* Texas Christian University Press. ISBN 0-87565-161-5.

Hamblin, Ken. 1997. *Pick a Better Country: An Unassuming Colored Guy Speaks His Mind about America.* Simon & Schuster. ISBN 0-6848431-8-8.

Hamilton, Dona Cooper, and Charles V. Hamilton. 1998. *The Dual Agenda: Race and Social Welfare Policies of Civil Rights Organizations.* Columbia University Press. ISBN 0-2311036-5-4.

Hamilton, Virginia. 1996. *Her Stories: African American Folk Tales, Fairy Tales and True Tales.* African American Images. ISBN 0-6142228-3-4.

Hardin, John A. 1997. *Fifty Years of Segregation: Black Higher Education in Kentucky, 1904–1954.* University Press of Kentucky. ISBN 0-8131202-4-1.

Harlan, Louis R. 1996. *All at Sea: Coming of Age in World War II.* University of Illinois Press. ISBN 0-252-02232-7.

Harris, Eddy L. 1999. *Still Life in Harlem.* Diane Publishing Company. ISBN 0-7881649-4-5.

Harris, Francis C., with Charles F. Harris, Jr. 1994. *The Amistad Pictorial History of the African American Athlete.* Amistad Press Inc. ISBN 1-56743-067-8.

Harris, Frederick C. 1999. *Something Within: Religion in African American Political Activism.* Oxford University Press. ISBN 0-1951203-3-7.

Harris, Jr., Robert L. 2000. *Teaching African American History.* American Historical Association. ISBN 0-8722906-6-2.

Harris, Paul. 1999. *Black Rage Confronts the Law.* New York University Press. ISBN 0-8147352-7-4.

Hartman, Chester, ed. 1996. *Double Exposure: Poverty and Race in America.* M.E. Sharpe. ISBN 1-56324-962-6.

Harvey, Paul. 1997. *Redeeming the South: Religious Cultures and Racial Identities among Southern Baptists, 1865–1925.* University of North Carolina Press. ISBN 0-8078232-4-4.

Haskins, James. 1999. *Distinguished African American Political and Governmental Leaders.* Greenwood Publishing Group. ISBN 1-57356-126-6.

Hauke, Kathleen A. 1999. *Ted Poston: Pioneer American Journalist.* Temple University Press. ISBN 0-8203-2020-X.

Hauser, Thomas, with Muhammad Ali. 1996. *Muhammad Ali: In Perspective.* HarperCollins. ISBN 0-0022518-9-2.

Hemphill, Paul. 2000. *The Ballad of Little River: A Tale of Race and Restless Youth in the Rural South.* Free Press. ISBN 0-6848568-2-4.

Henderson, Alex, ed. 1999. *Freedom's Odyssey: African-American History Essays from Phylon.* Clark Atlanta University. ISBN 0-9668555-0-7.

Henderson, Bill, ed. 1995. *The Pushcart Prize XXI: Best of the Small Presses.* Pushcart Press. ISBN 0-916-36696-0.

Henderson, George. 1999. *Our Souls to Keep: Black/White Relations in America.* Intercultural Press. ISBN 1-877864-65-X.

Henry, Charles P., ed. 1999. *Ralph Bunche: Model Negro or American Other?* New York University Press. ISBN 0-8147358-2-7.

Henry, Neil. 2001. *Pearl's Secret: A Black Man's Search for His White Family.* Univ. of California Press. ISBN 0-520-22257-1.

Herrnstein, Richard, and Charles Murray. 1994. *The Bell Curve: Intelligence and Class Structure in American Life.* Free Press. ISBN 0-0291467-3-9.

Higginbothom, Jr., A. Leon. 1998. *Shades of Freedom: Racial Politics and Presumptions of the American Legal Process.* Oxford University Press. ISBN 0-1951228-8-7.

Higginson, Thomas W. 1998. *Black Rebellion: Five Slave Revolts.* Da Capo Press. ISBN 0-3068086-7-6.

Higham, John, ed. 1997. *Civil Rights and Social Wrongs: Black-White Relations since World War II.* Penn State University Press. ISBN 0-271-01709-0.

Hill, Anita Faye. 1998. *Speaking Truth to Power.* Doubleday. ISBN 0-3854762-7-2.

Hill, Anita Faye, and Coleman, Emma. 1995. *Race, Gender, and Power in America. The Legacy of the Hill-Thomas Hearings.* Oxford University Press. ISBN 0-1950877-4-7.

Hill, Grant. 1997. *Change the Game: One Athlete's Thoughts on Sports, Dreams, and Growing Up.* Warner Books. ISBN 0-4466726-2-9.

Hilliard III, Asa G. 1994. *The Maroon within Us.* Black Classic Press. ISBN 0-933121-84-9.

Hine, Darlene Clark., ed. 1999. *A Question of Manhood: A Reader in U.S. Black Men's History and Masculinity.* Volume I: "Manhood Rights": The Construction of Black Male History, 1750–1870. Indiana University Press. ISBN 0-2533363-9-2.

Hine, Darlene Clark, and Kathleen Thompson. 1998. *A Shining Thread of Hope: The History of Black Women in America.* Broadway Books. ISBN 0-7679-0110-x.

Hinks, Peter P. 1996. *To Awaken My Afflicted Brethren: David Walker and the Problem of Antebellum Slave Resistance.* Penn State Press. ISBN 0-2710157-9-9.

Hobbs, Michael A. 1997. *Outcast: My Journey from the White House to Homelessness.* Middle Passage Press. ISBN 1-8810320-5-1.

Hoberman, John. 1997. *Darwin's Athletes: How Sport Has Damaged Black America and Preserved the Myth of Race.* Houghton Mifflin. ISBN 0-3958229-2-0.

Hobson, Fred. 1999. *But Now I See: The White Southern Racial Conversion.* Louisiana State University Press. ISBN 0-8071238-4-6.

Hodges, Craig, and Useni Eugene Perkins. 1996. *Beyond the Three Point Line.* Third World Press. ISBN 0-88378-161-1.

Holly, Ellen. 1998. *One Life: The Autobiography of an African-American Actress.* Kodansha America. ISBN 1-5683619-7-1.

Holmes, Larry, with Phil Berger. 1999. *Larry Holmes: Against the Odds.* St. Martin's Press. ISBN 0-3122461-4-5.

Holmes, Steven A. 2000. *Ron Brown: An Uncommon Life.* John Wiley. ISBN 0-4714017-2-2.

Holway, John B. 1997. *Red Tails, Black Wings: The Men of America's Black Air Force.* Yucca Tree. ISBN 1-881325-21-0.

Honigsberg, Peter J. 2000. *Crossing Border Street: A Civil Rights Memoir.* University of California Press. ISBN 0-5202214-7-8.

hooks, bell. 1996. *Killing Rage: Ending Racism.* Henry Holt. ISBN 08050272.

———. 1996. *Reel to Real: Race, Sex, and Class at the Movies.* Routledge. ISBN 0-415-91824-3.

———. 1997. *Bone Black: Memories of Girlhood.* Henry Holt. ISBN 0-8050551-2-6.

———. 1999. *Remembered Rapture: The Writer at Work.* Henry Holt. ISBN 0-8050-5909-1.

Hopson, Darlene P., and Derek S. Hopson. 1999. *The Power of Soul: Pathways to Psychological and Spiritual Growth for African Americans.* Morrow/Avon. ISBN 0-6881663-0-X.

Horowitz, David. 1999. *Hating Whitey: And Other Progressive Causes.* Spence Publishing. ISBN 1-8906262-1-X.

Howe, Stephen. 1998. *Afocentrism: Mythical Pasts and Imagined Homes.* Verso. ISBN 1-85984-873-7.

Hrabowski III, Freeman A., et al. 1998. *Beating the Odds: Raising Academically Successful African-American Males.* Oxford University Press. ISBN 0-19-510219-3.

Hudson, Wade, and Cheryl Hudson, comps. 1997. *In Praise of Our Fathes and Our Mothers: A Black Family Treasury by Outstanding Authors and Artists.* Just Us Books. ISBN 0-940975-59-9.

Huggins, Nathan, ed. 1999. *Whoopi Goldberg.* Chelsea House Publishers. ISBN 0-7910215-3-X.

Hunt, Annie Mae, and Ruthe Winegarten. 1996. *I Am Annie Mae: An Extraordinary Black Texas Woman in Her Own Words.* University of Texas Press. ISBN 0-2927909-9-6.

Hunt, Marsha. 1996. *Repossessing Ernestine: A Granddaughter Uncovers the Secret History of Her American Family.* HarperCollins. ISBN 0-0601744-3-9.

Hunter, Tera W. 1997. *To 'Joy My Freedom: Southern Black Women's Lives and Labors after the Civil War.* Harvard University Press. ISBN 0-6748930-9-3.

Hurd, Michael. 1998. *Black College Football, 1892–1992.* Donning Company. ISBN 1-57864-048-2.

Hutchinson, Earl Ofari. 1996. *The Assassination of the Black Male Image.* Simon & Schuster. ISBN 0-684-83100-7.

———. 1996. *Betrayed: A History of Presidential Failure to Protect Black Lives.* Westview Press. ISBN 0-8133246-5-3.

———. 1998. *The Crisis in Black and Black.* Middle Passage Press. ISBN 1-881032-14-0.

Jackson, Jesse. 1998. *Legal Lynching: Racism, Injustice and the Death Penalty.* Marlowe & Company. ISBN 1-5692470-6-4.

Jackson, Robert Scoop. 1995. *The Darkside: Chronicling the Young Black Experience.* Noble Press. ISBN 1-879360-40-3.

Jacobs, Bruce. 1999. *Race Manners: Navigating the Minefield between Black and White Americans.* Arcade Publishing. ISBN 1-5597045-3-5.

James, Joy. 1996. *Transcending the Talented Tenth: Black Leaders and American Intellectuals.* Routledge. ISBN 0-4159176-3-8.

James, Winston. 1998. *Holding Aloft the Banner of Ethiopia: Caribbean Radicalism in America.* Verso. ISBN 1-85984-999-7.

Jameson, Elizabeth, and Susan Armitage, eds. 1997. *Writing the Range: Race, Class, and Culture in the Women's West.* Univerity of Oklahoma Press. ISBN 0-8061295-2-2.

Jamison, Sandra Lee. 1999. *Finding Your People: An African American Guide to Discovering Your Roots.* Berkley Publishing Group. ISBN 0-3995247-8-9.

Janken, Kenneth Robert. 1997. *Rayford W. Logan and the Dilemma of the African American Intellectual.* University of Massachusetts Press. ISBN 1-5584906-9-8.

Jarrett, Hobart, S. 1995. *The History of Sigma Pi Phi: First of the African-American Greek-Letter Fraternities.* Quantum Leap Publisher. ISBN 0-9627161-8-9.

Jelloun, Tahar Ben. 2000. *Racism Explained to My Daughter.* New Press. ISBN 1-5658453-4-X.

Jett, Joseph, with Sabra Chartrand. 1999. *Black and White on Wall Street: The Untold Story of the Man Wrongly Accused of Bringing Down Kidder Peabody.* Morrow. ISBN 0-688-16136-7.

Johnson, Alonzo, and Paul Jersild, eds. 1996. *"Ain't Gonna Lay My 'Ligion Down": African American Religion.* University of South Carolina Press. ISBN 1-5700310-9-6.

Johnson, Charles, Patricia Smith, and WGBH Series Research Team. 1998. *Africans in America: America's Journey through Slavery.* Harcourt Brace. ISBN 0-15-100339-4.

Johnson, Dorothy Sharpe, and Lula Goolsby William. n.d. *Pioneering Women of the African Methodist Episcopal Zion Church 1796–1996.* A.M.E. Zion Publishing House. INA.

Johnson, Ernest. 1999. *Brothers on the Mend: Understanding and Healing Anger for African American Men and Women.* Pocket Books. ISBN 0-6715114-6-7.

Johnson, Jesse J. 1978. *Roots of Two Black Marine Sergeants Major: Profiles in Courage.* Carver Publishing. ISBN 0-9150441-3-7.

Johnson, Michael. 1997. *Slaying the Dragon.* Smithmark Publishers. ISBN 0-7651065-7-4.

Johnson, Walter. 2001. *Soul by Soul: Life inside the Antebellum Slave Market.* Harvard University Press. ISBN 0-6740053-9-2.

Johnson, Whittington B. 1999. *Black Savannah: 1788–1864.* University of Arkansas Press. ISBN 1-5572854-6-2.

Johnson-Hall, Wanda. In press. *Telling the Truth and Shaming the Devil.* Ewanston Press. ISBN 1-8792604-0-9.

Jolley, Willie. 1997. *It Only Takes a Minute to Change Your Life!* St. Martin's Press. ISBN 0-312-96110-3.

Jones, Bobby, and Lesley Sussman. 1998. *Touched by God: America's Gospel Greats Share Their Stories of Finding God.* Pocket Books. ISBN 0-6710200-2-1.

Jones, Charles, ed. 1998. *The Black Panther Party Reconsidered.* Black Classic Press. ISBN 0-933121-96-2.

Jones, Deacon, and John Slawitter. 1996. *Headslap: The Life and Times of Deacon Jones.* Prometheus Books. ISBN 1-5739208-2-7.

Jones, Howard. 1997. *Mutiny on the "Amistad."* Oxford University Press. ISBN 0-1950382-9-0.

Jones, Lee, ed. 2000. *Brothers of the Academy: Up and Coming Black Scholars Earning Our Way in Higher Education.* Stylus. ISBN 1-57922-028-2.

————, ed. 2000. *Retraining African Americans in Higher Education: Challenging Paradigms for Retaining Black Students, Faculty and Administrators.* Stylus Publishers. ISBN 1-579220428.

Jones, William. 1998. *Is God a White Racist?* Beacon Press. ISBN 0-8070103-3-2.

Jordan, June. 1998. *Affirmative Acts: Political Essays.* Doubleday/Anchor. ISBN 0-3854922-5-1.

Joyner-Kersee, Jackie, with Sonja Steptoe. 1997. *A Kind of Grace: The Autobiography of the World's Greatest Female Athlete.* Warner Books. ISBN 0-446-52248-1.

Jules-Rosette, Bennetta. 2000. *Black Paris: The African Writers' Landscape.* University of Illinois Press. ISBN 0-2520693-5-8.

Kahlenberg, Richard D. 1996. *The Remedy: Class Race, and Affirmative Action.* New Republic Book/Basic Books. ISBN 0-6149574-6-x.

Karim, Benjamin, with Peter Skutches and David Gallen. 1995. *Remembering Malcolm.* Ballantine Publishing Group. ISBN 0-3454005-1-8.

Katz, William Loren. 1995. *Black Women of the Old West.* Atheneum Books for Young Readers. ISBN 0-6893194-4-4.

Katz, William Loren. 1997. *Black Legacy: A History of New York's African-Americans.* Atheneum. ISBN 0-6893191-3-4.

Kaufman, Kenneth C. 1996. *Dred Scott's Advocate: A Biography of Roswell M. Field.* University of Missouri Press. ISBN 0-8262109-2-9.

Keiler, Allan. 2000. *Marian Anderson, a Singer's Journey: The First Comprehensive Biography.* Scribner. ISBN 0-6848071-1-4.

Kelley, Robin D. G., and Earl Lewis. 2000. *To Make Our World Anew: A History of African Americans.* Oxford University Press. ISBN 0-1951394-5-3.

Kenan, Randall. 1999. *Walking on Water: Black American Lives at the Turn of the Twenty-first Century.* Knopf. ISBN 0-679-40827-4.

Kennedy, Randall. 1997. *Race, Crime, and the Law.* Pantheon. ISBN 0-679-43881-5.

Key, William J, and Robert Johnson Smith II. 1996. *From One Brother to Another: Voices of African-American Men.* Judson Press. ISBN 0-8170125-0-8.

Kilgore, Jr., Thomas, with Jini Kilgore Ross. 1996. *God's Glory, Humanity's Praise: Materials for Worship and Meditation.* Beckham House Publishers. ISBN 0-9317614-5-x.

Kincaid, Jamaica. 1998. *My Brother.* Farrar, Straus & Giroux. ISBN 0-3745256-2-5.

King, B. B., with David Ritz. 1999. *Blues All around Me: The Autobiography of B. B. King.* Morrow/Avon. ISBN 0-3808076-0-2.

King, Bernice, Rev. 1998. *Hard Questions, Heart Answers: Sermons and Speeches.* Broadway Books. ISBN 0-5530692-1-7.

King, Desmond. 2000. *Making Americans: Immigration, Race, and the Origins of the Diverse Democracy.* Harvard University Press. ISBN 0-6740008-8-9.

King, Jr., Martin L. 1964. *Why We Can't Wait.* New American Library. ISBN 0-4516275-4-7.

———. n.d. *The Autobiography of Martin Luther King, Jr.* Edited by Clayborne Carson, Jr. Warner Books. ISBN 0-4466765-0-0.

King, Wilma. 1995. *Stolen Childhood: Slave Youth in Nineteenth-Century America.* Indiana University Press. ISBN 0-253-32904-3.

Klammer, Martin. 1997. *Whitman, Slavery, and the Emergence of "Leaves of Grass."* Penn State Press. ISBN 0-2710164-2-6.

Knight, Gladys. 1998. *Between Each Line of Pain and Glory: My Life Story.* Hyperion. ISBN 0-7868837-1-5.

Knupfer, Anne Meis. 1997. *Toward a Tenderer Humanity and a Nobler Womanhood: African American Women's Clubs in Turn-of-the-Century Chicago.* New York University Press. ISBN 0-8147469-1-8.

Kohn, Howard. 1998. *We Had a Dream: A Tale of the Struggle for Integration in America.* Simon & Schuster. ISBN 0-6848087-4-9.

Kornweibel, Jr., Theodore. 1999. *Seeing Red: Federal Campaigns against Black Militancy, 1919–1925.* Indiana University Press. ISBN 0-2532135-4-1.

Kotlowitz, Alex. 1999. *The Other Side of the River.* Doubleday. ISBN 0-3854722-1-X.

Krang, Rachel, and Philip J. Koslow. 1999. *The Biographical Dictionary of African Americans.* Checkmark Books. ISBN 0-8160-3904-6.

Kreuter, Gretchen Von Loewe. 1996. *Forgotten Promise: Race and Gender Wars on a Small College Campus.* Edited by Jan Garrett. Knopf. ISBN 0-679-44700-8.

Kromer, Helen. 1988. *"Amistad": The Slave Uprising aboard the Spanish Schooner.* United Church Press. ISBN 0-8298126-5-2.

Kunjufu, Jawanza. 1998. *Black College Student Survival Guide.* African American Images. ISBN 0-9135435-5-1.

Labelle, Patti. 1998. *Don't Block the Blessings.* Berkley Publishing Group. ISBN 0-4251699-8-7.

Ladner, Joyce A., ed. 1998. *The Death of White Sociology.* Black Classic Press. ISBN 1-5747800-8-5.

Laird, Jr., Roland, and Taneshia Nash Laird. 1997. *Still I Rise: A Cartoon History of African Americans.* Norton. ISBN 0-393-04538-2.

Lamy, Philip. 1996. *Millennium Rage: Survivalists, White Supremacists, and the Doomsday Prophecy.* Perseus Publishing. ISBN 0-306-45409-2.

Landrum, Gene N. 1997. *Profiles of Black Success: Thirteen Creative Geniuses Who Changed the World.* Prometheus Books. ISBN 1-57392-119-x.

Landsman, Julie. n.d. *A White Teacher Talks about Race.* Scarecrow. ISBN 1-5788-6013-x.

Lanning, Michael Lee. 1999. *The African-American Soldier: From Crispus Attucks to Colin Powell.* Carol Publishing/Birch Lane. ISBN 0-8065204-9-3.

Lathan, E. Lemay. 1997. *The Black Man's Guide to Working in the White Man's World.* General Publishing Group. ISBN 1-5754405-1-2.

Lavin, David, and David Hyllegard. 1996. *Changing the Odds: Open Admissions and the Life Chances of the Disadvantaged.* Yale University Press. ISBN 0-3000632-8-8.

Law, Bob. 1998. *Voices from the Future: A Contemporary Look at African Wisdom That Provides a Blueprint for the Future.* African American Images. ISBN 0-9135435-7-8.

Lawrence-Lightfoot, Sarah. 1994. *I've Known Rivers: Lives of Loss and Liberation.* Addison-Wesley. ISBN 0-201-58120-5.

————. 1999. *Respect: An Exploration.* Perseus/Merloyd Lawrence. ISBN 0-7382-0093-x.

Lazarre, Jane. 1996. *Beyond the Whiteness of Whiteness: Memoir of a White Mother of Black Sons.* Duke University Press. ISBN 0-8223-1826-1.

Lazo, Caroline. 1994. *Martin Luther King Jr.* Silver Burdett Ginn. ISBN 0-87518-618-1.

Lee, Elaine, ed. 1998. *Go Girl: The Black Woman's Book of Travel and Adventure.* Eighth Mountain Press. ISBN 0-9333774-3-6.

Lee, Spike. 1998. *The Best Seat in the House.* Crown. ISBN 0-6098019-1-0.

Leeming, David. 1998. *Amazing Grace: A Life of Beauford Delaney.* Oxford University Press. ISBN 0-1950978-4-x.

Lefkowitz, Mary. 1997. *Not Out of Africa: How Afrocentrism Became an Excuse to Teach Myth as History.* New Republic Book/Basic Books. ISBN 0-4650983-8-x.

Lefkowitz, Mary R., and Guy M. Rogers, eds. 1996. *Black Athena Revisited.* University of North Carolina Press. ISBN 0-8078455-5-8.

Lemann, Nicholas. 1992. *The Promised Land: The Great Black Migration and How It Changed America.* David McKay. ISBN 0-6797334-7-7.3

Lester, Julius. 2000. *Sam and the Tigers.* Dial. ISBN 0-1405628-8-5.

Levine, Robert S. 1997. *Martin Delany, Frederick Douglass, and the Politics of Representative Identity.* University of North Carolina Press. ISBN 0-8078463-3-3.

Levinsohn, Florence H. 1997. *Looking for Farrakhan.* Ivan R. Dee. ISBN 1-56663-157-2.

Lewis, David Levering. 1997. *When Harlem Was in Vogue.* Penguin. ISBN 0-1402633-4-9.

Lewis, Earl, and Heidi Ardizzone. 2000. *Love on Trial: An American Scandal in Black and White.* Norton. ISBN 0-393050130.

Lewis, John, and Michael D'Orso. 1998. *Walking with the Wind: A Memoir of the Movement.* Simon & Schuster. ISBN 0-684-81065-4.

Lincoln, C. Eric. 1996. *Coming through the Fire: Surviving Race and Place in America.* Duke University Press. ISBN 0-8223173-6-2.

———. 1999. *Race, Religion and the Continuing American Dilemma.* Hill & Wang. ISBN 089016230.

Linderman, Gerald F. 1999. *The World within War. America's Combat Experience in World War II.* Harvard University Press. ISBN 0-6749620-2-8.

Litwack, Leon F. 1998. *Trouble in Mind: Black Southerners in the Age of Jim Crow.* Knopf. ISBN 0-394-52778-x.

Livingston, Michael E. 1997. *The African-American Book of Lists.* Perigee. ISBN 0-1642536-1-6.

Loizeaux, William. 1997. *The Shooting of Rabbit Wells: An American Tragedy.* Arcade Publishing. ISBN 1-5597038-0-6.

Lopez, Ian. 1997. *White by Law: The Legal Constitution of Race.* New York University Press. ISBN 0-8147513-7-7.

Lott, Tommy L. 1999. *The Invention of Race: Black Culture and the Politics of Representation.* Blackwell Publishers. ISBN 0-631-21018-0.

Love, Spencie. 1996. *One Blood: The Death and Resurrection of Charles R. Drew.* University of North Carolina Press. ISBN 0-8078225-0-7.

Lowe, Janet C., and Oprah Winfrey. 1998. *Oprah Winfrey Speaks: Insight From the World's Most Influential Voice.* John Wiley. ISBN 0-471-29864-6.

Lubiano, Wahneema. 1999. *The House That Race Built.* Random House. ISBN 0-5173616-4-7.

Luttery, Kevin. 1997. *A Stranger in My Bed.* Bryant & Dillon Publishers. ISBN 1-8894080-3-4.

Lynn, Conrad. 1993. *There Is a Fountain: The Autobiography of Conrad Lynn.* Chicago Review Press. ISBN 1-5565216-6-9.

Mabokela, Reitumetse Obakeng, ed. 2001. *Sisters of the Academy: Emergent Black Women Scholars in Higher Education.* Foreword by Bertice Berry. Stylus Publishers. ISBN 1-57922038x.

Mabry, Marcus. 1995. *White Bucks and Black-Eyed Peas: Coming of Age Black in White America.* Simon & Schuster. ISBN 0-6841966-9-7.

Madhubuti, Haki R. 1978. *Enemies: The Clash of Races.* Third World Press. ISBN 0-88378-073-9.

Madison, Joseph E. 1997. *Black Man's Hell: From Slavery to the CIA-Crack Connection.* Marlowe & Company. ISBN 1-56924-712-9.

Magida, Arthur J. 1997. *Prophet of Rage: A Life of Louis Farrakhan and His Nation.* Foreword by Julian Bond. Basic Books. ISBN 04650637x.

Magnin, Andre, and Jacques Soulillou, eds. 1996. *Contemporary Art of Africa.* Abrams. ISBN 0-8109-4032-9.

Maier, Karl. 1999. *Into the House of the Ancestors: Inside the New Africa.* John Wiley. ISBN 0-4712958-3-3.

Majozo, Estella C. 1999. *Come Out of the Wilderness: Memoir of a Black Woman Artist.* Feminist Press. ISBN 1-5586120-6-8.

Manning, M. M. 1998. *Slave in a Box: The Strange Career of Aunt Jemima (The American South Series).* University Press of Virginia. ISBN 0-8139181-1-1.

————. 1997. *Black Liberation in Conservative America.* South End. ISBN 0-89608-560-0.

————. 1998. *Black Leadership.* Columbia University Press. ISBN 0-231-10746-3.

————. 1998. *Speaking Truth to Power: Essays on Race, Resistance, and Radicalism.* Westview Press. ISBN 0-8133882-8-7.

Marcus, Laurence R. 1996. *Fighting Words: The Politics of Hateful Speech.* Praeger. ISBN 0-275-95438-2.

Markowitz, Gerald, and David Rosner. 1996. *Children, Race, and Power: Kenneth and Mamie Clark's North-Side Center.* University Press of Virginia. ISBN 0-8139-1687-9.

Marsh, Charles. 1999. *God's Long Summer: Stories of Faith and Civil Rights.* Princeton University Press. ISBN 0-6910294-0-7.

———. n.d. *Last Days: Purity and Peril in a Small Southern Town.* Basic. ISBN 0-465-04418-2.

Marshall, A. 1995. *Louis Farrakhan: Made in America.* BSB Publishing. ISBN 0-9645729-00.

Marshall, Jr., Joseph, and Lonnie Wheeler. 1997. *Street Soldier: One Man's Struggle to Save a Generation—One Life at a Time.* Doubleday. ISBN 0-3853170-6-9.

Martin, Reginald. 1999. *Dark Eros: Black Erotic Writings.* St. Martin's Press. ISBN 0-3121985-0-7.

Mason, Jr., Herman. 1999. *The Talented Tenth: The Founders and Presidents of Alpha.* Four-G Publishers. ISBN 185066635.

Masters, Jarvis. 1997. *Seeking Silences.* Parallax. ISBN 0-6142798-2-8.

Matsuda, Mari J. 1996. *Where Is Your Body? And Other Essays on Race, Gender and the Law.* Beacon Press. ISBN 0-8070-6780-6.

Matsuoka, Fumitaka. 1998. *Color of Faith: Building Community in a Multiracial Society.* United Church Press. ISBN 0-8298128-1-4.

Mattavous-Bly, Viola. 1997. *African Connections.* Vantage Press. ISBN 0-5331214-1-8.

Mayer, Jane, and Jill Abramson. 1995. *Strange Justice: The Selling of Clarence Thomas.* Dutton/Plume. ISBN 0-4522749-9-0.

Maynard, Robert C., with Dori J. Maynard. 1995. *Letters to My Children.* Andrews & McMeel. ISBN 0-8362702-7-4.

McBride, James. 1996. *The Color of Water: A Black Man's Tribute to His White Mother.* G. P. Putnam's Sons. ISBN 1-5732202-2-1.

McCall, Nathan. 1998. *What's Going On?* Vintage Books. ISBN 0-3757015-0-8.

McClain, Leanita, and Clarence Page. 1995. *What Killed Leanita McClain? Essays in Living in Both Black and White Worlds.* Noble Press. ISBN 1-879360-38-1.

McCluskey, Audrey, and Elaine Smith, eds. 1999. *Mary McLeod Bethune: Building a Better World.* Indiana University Press. ISBN 0-2533362-6-0.

McCray, Carrie Allen. 1999. *The Life of a Confederate General's Black Daughter.* Algonquin Book of Chapel Hill/Workman. ISBN 1-56512-186-4.

McDaniel, Betty F. n.d. *Man with a Vision: Bishop Arthur M. Brazier.* Lithicolor Press.

McDowell, Deborah E. 1998. *Leaving Pipe Shop: Memories of Kin.* Norton. ISBN 0-3933184-3-5.

McElrath, Jr., Joseph R., and Robert C. Leitz. 1996. *To Be an Author: Letters of Charles W. Chestnutt, 1889–1905.* Princeton University Press. ISBN 0-6910366-8-3.

McGary, Howard. 1998. *Race and Social Justice.* Blackwell Publishers. ISBN 0-631-20721-X.

McGivern, Gene, and Dennis Green. 1997. *Dennis Green: No Room for Crybabies.* Sports Publishing. ISBN 1-5716717-5-7.

McGreevy, John T. 1998. *Parish Boundaries: The Catholic Encounter with Race in the Twentieth-Century North.* University of Chicago Press. ISBN 0-2265587-4-6.

McKenzie, Vashti M. 1996. *Not without a Struggle: Leadership Development for African Women in Ministry.* Pilgrim Press/United Church Press. ISBN 0-8298107-6-5.

McKnight, Reginald. 1999. *White Boys and Other Stories.* Henry Holt. ISBN 0-8050617-1-1.

McMurray, George, and Ndugu T'Ofori-Atta. n.d. *The Birth of a Denomination: The Story of Mother Zion African Methodist Episcopal Zion Church, 200 Years of Evangelism and Liberation.* A.M.E. Zion Publishing House.

McMurry, Linda O. 1999. *To Keep the Waters Troubled: The Life of Ida B. Wells.* Oxford University Press. ISBN 0-19-508812-3.

McPherson, James Alan. 1999. *Crabcakes: A Memoir.* Simon & Schuster. ISBN 06847965.

McWhirter, Darien. 1996. *The End of Affirmative Action: Where Do We Go from Here?* Carol Publishing Group. ISBN 1-55972-339-4.

Meacham, Virginia. 1998. *Chained to the Rock of Adversity: To Be Free, Black, and Female in the Old South.* University of Georgia Press. ISBN 0-8203208-3-8.

Meredith, Martin. 1999. *Nelson Mandela.* St. Martin's Press. ISBN 0-3121999-2-9.

Mfume, Kweisi. 1997. *No Free Ride: From the Mean Streets to the Mainstream.* Ballantine/One World. ISBN 0-3454136-4-4.

Milano, Susan Murphy. 1995. *Defending Our Lives: Protecting Yourself from Stalking and Domestic Violence.* Noble Press. ISBN 1-879360-41-1.

Miles, Johnnie L., et al. 2001. *The Slave Trade: The Story of the Atlantic Slave Trade, 1440–1870.* Prentice Hall Press. ISBN 0-7352-0226-5.

Miller, Davis. 1999. *The Tao of Muhammad Ali: A True Story.* Crown. ISBN 0-6098045-3-7.

Miller, E. Ethelbert. 2000. *Fathering Words: The Making of an African American Writer.* St. Martin's Press. ISBN 0-3122413-6-4.

Miller, Jerome G. 1996. *Search and Destroy: African-American Males in the Criminal Justice System.* Cambridge University. ISBN 0-521-46021-2.

Miller, Norma, with Evette Jensen. 2001. *Swingin' at the Savoy: The Memoir of a Jazz Dancer.* Temple University Press. ISBN 1-5663984-9-5.

Miller, Robert. 1994. *The Story of Nat Love.* Silver Burdett Ginn. ISBN 0-382-24390-0.

Miller, William Lee. 1998. *Arguing about Slavery: The Great Battle in the United States Congress.* Vintage Books. ISBN 0-6797684-4-0.

Millner, Denene. 1997. *The Sistahs' Rules: Not to Be Confused with "The Rules."* HarperTrade. ISBN 0-688-15689-4.

Millner, Denene, and Nick Chiles. 1999. *What Brothers Think, What Sistahs Know: The Real Deal on Love and Relationships.* Harper-Trade. ISBN 0-688-16498-6.

Mills, Charles W. 1997. *The Racial Contract.* Cornell University Press. ISBN 0-8014-3454-8.

Minerbrook, Scott. 1996. *Divided to the Vein: A Journey into Race and Family.* Harcourt Trade. ISBN 0-15-193107-0.

Mitchell, Angela. 1998. *What the Blues Is All About.* Berkley Publishing Group. ISBN 0-3995237-6-6.

Moore, N. 1997. *Pulpit Confessions: Exposing the Black Church.* Exodus Books. ISBN 0-9658299-2-8.

Morgan, Philip D. 1998. *Slave Counterpoint: Black Culture in the Eighteenth-Century Chesapeake and Lowcountry.* University of North Carolina Press. ISBN 0-8078240-9-7.

Morris, Willie. 1999. *The Ghosts of Medgar Evers: A Tale of Race, Murder, Mississippi and Hollywood.* Random House. ISBN 0-5173696-9-9.

Morrison, Toni, and Claudia Brodsky Lacour, eds. 1997. *Birth of a Nation'hood: Gaze, Script and Spectacle in the O. J. Simpson Case.* Pantheon. ISBN 0-6797589-3-3.

Mosely, Walter. 2000. *Workin' on the Chain Gang: Shaking Off the Dead Hand of History.* Ballantine Publishing Group. ISBN 0-3454306-9-7.

Mosely, Walter, Manthia Diawara, and Clyde Taylor, eds. 1999. *Black Genius: African American Solutions to African American Problems.* Norton. ISBN 0-3930470-1-6.

Moses, Greg. 1998. *Revolution of Conscience: Martin Luther King, Jr.* Guilford Publications. ISBN 1-5723040-7-3.

Moskos, Charles C., and John Sibley Butler. 1997. *All That We Can Be: Black Leadership and Racial Integration the Army Way.* Basic Books. ISBN 0-4650011-3-0.

Mumford, Kevin J. 1997. *Interzones: Black/White Sex Districts in Chicago and New York in the Early Twentieth Century.* Columbia University Press. ISBN 0-2311049-3-6.

Mustafa, Al. 1996. *Alif Lam Ra: The Path to the Hereafter.* WriteMore Publications. ISBN 1-887798-00-5.

Myrdal, Gunnar. 1996. *An American Dilemma: The Negro Problem and Modern Democracy (Black and African American Studies).* Reprint edition, vol. 1. Transaction Publishers. ISBN 1-5600085-6-3.

Nalty, Bernard C. 1997. *The Right to Fight: African-American Marines in World War II.* Gordon Press Publishers. ISBN 0-8490608-3-4.

Nash, Gary B. 1990. *Race and Revolution.* Rowman & Littlefield Publishers. ISBN 0-945612-11-7.

Nash, Sunny. 1997. *Bigmama Didnt Shop at Woolworth's.* Texas A&M University Press. ISBN 0-8909671-6-4.

Neblett, Pat. 1996. *Circles of Sisterhood: A Book Discussion Group Guide for Women of Color.* Writers and Readers. ISBN 0-8631624-5-2.

Nelson, Jill. 1999. *Straight No Chaser: How I Became a Grown-Up Black Woman.* Penguin Putnam. ISBN 0-1402772-4-2.

Nevins, Beatryce. 1998. *Success Strategies for African-Americans.* Dutton/Plume. ISBN 0-452-27524-5.

Newman, Richard. 1999. *Go Down, Moses: A Celebration of the African American Spiritual.* Random House. ISBN 0-5174276-2-1.

Newton, Adolph. 1999. *Newton, Adolph, Better than Good: A Black Sailor's War, 1943–1945.* Naval Institute Press. ISBN 1-5575064-9-3.

Newton, Mack, and Michele St. George. 1997. *A Path to Power: A Master's Guide to Conquering Crisis.* NTKD Publishing. ISBN 0-9659821-3-0.

Nicholson, Stuart. 1995. *Billie Holiday.* Northeastern University Press. ISBN 1-55553-303-5.

———. 1995. *Ella Fitzgerald: A Biography of the First Lady of Jazz.* Capo Press. ISBN 0-3068064-2-8.

Nickson, Chris. 1996. *Denzel Washington.* St. Martin's Press. ISBN 0-3129604-3-3.

Nikuradse, Tamara. 1997. *My Mother Had a Dream.* Dutton/Plume. ISBN 0-4522760-5-5.

————, ed. 1998. *African-American Wedding Readings.* New American Library. ISBN 0-525-94403-6.

Njeri, Itabari. 1997. *The Last Plantation: Color, Conflict, and Identity: Reflections of a New World Black.* Houghton Mifflin. ISBN 0-395-77191-9.

Norman, Teresa. 1998. *The African American Baby Name Book.* Berkley Publishing Group. ISBN 0-4251593-9-6.

Oakes, James. n.d. *The Ruling Race: A History of American Slaveholders.* Norton. ISBN 0-3933170-5-6.

Oakley, Giles. n.d. *The Devil's Music: A History of the Blues.* Da Capo Press. ISBN 0-3068074-3-2.

Oates, Stephen. n.d. *The Approaching Fury: Voices of the Storm, 1820–1861.* HarperCollins. ISBN 0-06-016784-x.

Obama, Barack. n.d. *Dreams from My Father: A Story of Race and Inheritance.* Kodansha America. ISBN 1-5683616-2-9.

Okwu, Julian C. R. 1997. *Face Forward: Young African-American Men in a Critical Age.* Chronicle. ISBN 0-8118-1631-1.

Oliver, Melvin, and Thomas M. Shapiro. 1996. *Black Wealth/White Wealth: A New Perspective on Racial Inequality.* Routledge. ISBN 0-4159184-7-2.

Olson, Lynn. n.d. *Freedom's Daughters: The Unsung Heroines of the Civil Rights Movement from 1830–1970.* Scribner. ISBN 0-684-85012-5.

Orfield, Gary, Susan E. Eaton, and Harvard Project on School Desegregation. 1997. *Dismantling Desegregation: The Quiet Reversal of Brown v. Board of Education.* New Press. ISBN 1-5658440-1-7.

Osofsky, Gilbert. 1996. *Harlem: The Making of a Ghetto: Negro New York, 1890–1930.* Ivan R. Dee. ISBN 1-5666310-4-1.

Owens, William. 1997. *Black Mutiny.* Dutton/Plume. ISBN 0-4522793-5-6.

Page, Clarence. 1997. *Showing My Color.* HarperTrade. ISBN 0-0609280-1-8.

Painter, Nell Irvin. 1996. *Sojourner Truth: A Life, A Symbol.* Norton. ISBN 0-393-02739-2.

Parish, James Robert. 1997. *Whoopi Goldberg: Her Journey from Poverty to Mega-Stardom.* Carol Publishing Group. ISBN 1-55972-431-5.

Parker, Gwendolyn M. 1999. *Trespassing: My Sojourn in the Halls of Privilege.* Houghton Mifflin. ISBN 0-3959262-0-3.

Parker, John P., and Stuart Sprague, eds. 1998. *His Promised Land: The Autobiography of John P. Parker, Former Slave and Conductor on the Underground Railroad.* Norton. ISBN 0-3933171-8-8.

Parker, Star, and Lorenzo Benet. 1998. *Pimps, Whores and Welfare Brats: The Stunning Conservative Transformation of a Former Welfare Queen.* Pocket Books. ISBN 0-6715346-6-1.

Patillo-Beals, Melba. 1999. *White Is a State of Mind.* Penguin USA. ISBN 0-3991446-4-1.

Patterson, Jerry R. In press. *The Hand of Fate.* Vantage Press. .

Patterson, Orlando. 1997. *The Ordeal of Integration: Progress and Resentment in America's Racial Crisis.* Counterpoint. ISBN 1-887178-61-9.

———. 1998. *Rituals of Blood: Defining the Color Line in Modern America.* Counterpoint. ISBN 1-8871788-2-1.

Patterson, Sharon C. 2000. *New Faith: A Black Christian Woman's Guide to Reformation, Re-creation, Rediscovery, Renaissance, Resurrection, and Revival.* Augsburg Fortress Publishers. ISBN 0-8006315-8-7.

Pegues, Lillian. 1998. *Family Tales: Curse or Happenstance?* Noble House. ISBN 1-56167-392-7.

Pemberton, Gale. 1992. *The Hottest Water in Chicago: On Family, Race, Time, and American Culture.* Faber & Faber. ISBN 0-571-12936-6.

Pepper, William F. 1998. *Orders to Kill: The Truth behind the Murder of Martin Luther King.* Warner Books. ISBN 0-4466739-4-3.

Percelay, James. 1998. *SNAPS 4.* William Morrow. ISBN 0-6881501-4-4.

Perry, Huey L. 1997. *Race, Politics, and Governance in the United States.* University Press of Florida. ISBN 0-8130148-1-6.

Petersen, Frank E., with J. Alfred Phelps. 1998. *Into the Tiger's Jaw: America's First Black Marine Aviator: The Autobiography of Lt. Gen. Frank E. Petersen.* Presidio Press. ISBN 0-89141-675-7.

Pettiway, Leon E. 1996. *Honey, Honey, Miss Thang: Being Black, Gay and on the Streets.* Temple University Press. ISBN 1-56639-498-8.

Phelts, Marsha Dean. 1997. *An American Beach for African Americans.* University of Florida. ISBN 0-8130-1504-9.

Pierce-Baker, Charlotte. 1998. *Surviving the Silence: Black Women's Stories of Rape.* Norton. ISBN 0-393-04661-3.

Piersen, William D., and Robert L. Harris, Jr. eds. 1997. *From Africa to America: African-American History from the Colonial Era to the Early Republic, 1526–1790.* Macmillan Library Reference. ISBN 0-8057390-3-3.

Pinderhughes, Howard. 1997. *Race in the Hood: Conflict and Violence among Youth.* University of Minnesota Press. ISBN 0-8166-2918-8.

Pinn, Anthony. 1998. *Varieties of African American Religious Experience.* Fortress. ISBN 0-8006299-4-9.

Poe, Richard. 1999. *Black Spark, White Fire.* Primal Publishing. ISBN 0-7615216-3-1.

Poinsett, Alex. 2000. *Walking with Presidents: Louis Martin and the Rise of Black Political Power.* Rowman & Littlefield Publishers. ISBN 0-8476974-1-x.

Poitier, Sidney. 2000. *The Measure of a Man: A Spiritual Autobiography.* Harper San Francisco. ISBN 0-0625160-7-8.

Pomerantz, Gary M. 1999. *Where Peachtree Meets Sweet Auburn: The Saga of Two Families and the Making of Atlanta.* Diane Publishing Company. ISBN 0-7881670-8-1.

Ponder, Rhinold L., and Michele Tuck-Ponder. 1996. *The Wisdom of the Word.* Random House. ISBN 0-5177059-1-5.

———, comp. 1996. *The Wisdom of the Word: Faith.* Crown. ISBN 0-6141979-8-8.

———, comp. 1997. *The Wisdom of the Word: Love.* Random House. ISBN 0-5177059-2-3.

Porter, Kenneth W. 1996. *The Black Seminoles: History of a Freedom-Seeking People.* University Press of Florida. ISBN 0-8130145-1-4.

Porter, Michael. 1998. *Kill Them before They Grow: The Misdiagnosis of African American Boys in America's Classrooms.* African American Images. ISBN 0-9135435-4-3.

Post, Robert, and Michael Rogin. 1998. *Race and Representation: Affirmative Action.* Zone Books. ISBN 0-942299-49-3.

Potter, Joan, and Constance Claytor. 1994. *African American Firsts.* Pinto Press.

Powell, Colin L. 1995. *My American Journey.* Random House. ISBN 0-679-43296-5.

Powell, Kevin. 1998. *Keepin' It Real: Post-MTV Reflections on Race, Sex, and Politics.* Ballantine Publishing Group. ISBN 0-3454247-8-6.

Powell, Richard J. 1997. *Black Art and Culture in the 20th Century.* Thames & Hudson. ISBN 0-5002029-5-8.

Powell, Richard, et al. 1997. *Rhapsodies in Black: Art of the Harlem Renaissance.* University of California Press. ISBN 0-5202126-8-1.

Proctor, Samuel DeWitt. 1996. *The Substance of Things Hoped For: A Memoir of African-American Faith.* Penguin Putnam. ISBN 0-399-14089-1.

Pryor, T. M. 1995. *Wealth Building Lessons of Booker T. Washington.* Duncan & Duncan Publishers. ISBN 1-878647-21-0.

Pullen, M. K. n.d. *Great Black Writers: Eight Profiles.* Open Hand Press.

Quarles, Benjamin. 1997. *Frederick Douglass.* Da Capo Press. ISBN 0-3068079-0-4.

Rampersad, Arnold. 1997. *Jackie Robinson: A Biography.* Knopf. ISBN 0-6794449-5-5.

Raybon, Patricia. 1996. *My First White Friend: Confessions on Race, Love and Forgiveness.* Viking. ISBN 0-670-85956-7.

Reddy, Maureen T. 1996. *Crossing the Color Line: Race, Parenting, and Culture.* Rutgers University Press. ISBN 0-8135237-4-5.

Reed, Jr., Adolph. 1999. *Stirrings in the Jug: Black Politics in the Post-segregation Era.* University of Minnesota Press. ISBN 0-8166268-0-4.

————. 1999. *W.E.B. Du Bois and American Political Thought: Fabianism and The Color Line.* Oxford University Press. ISBN 0-1951309-8-7.

————. 2001. *Class Notes.* New Press. ISBN 1-5658467-5-3.

Reed, Ishmael, ed. 1998. *Multi America: Essays on Cultural Wars and Cultural Peace.* Viking Penguin. ISBN 0-1402591-2-0.

Reese, Della. 1998. *Angels along the Way: My Life with Help from Above.* Boulevard Books. ISBN 0-4251657-3-6.

Reid-Merritt, Patricia. 1997. *Sister Power. How Phenomenal Black Women Are Rising to the Top.* John Wiley. ISBN 0-4711935-5-0.

Remick, David. 1998. *King of the World: Muhammad Ali and the Rise of an American Hero.* Random House. ISBN 0-375-50065-0.

Rhea, Joseph Tilden. 2001. *Race and Pride and the American Identity.* Harvard University Press. ISBN 0-6740057-6-7.

Rhines, Jesse Algeron. 1996. *Black Film, White Money.* Rutgers University Press. ISBN 0-8135-2267-6.

Rhodes, Jane. 2000. *Mary Ann Shadd Cary: The Black Press and Protest in the Nineteenth Century.* Indiana University Press. ISBN 0-2532135-0-9.

Richardson, James. 1997. *Willie Brown: Style, Power, and a Passion for Politics.* University of California Press. ISBN 0-5202131-5-7.

Richardson, Marilyn, ed. 1987. *Maria W. Stewart, America's First Black Political Writer.* Indiana University Press. ISBN 0-2533634-2-x.

Richardson, Willie. 1996. *Reclaiming the Urban Family: How to Mobilize the Church as a Family Training Center.* Zondervan Publishing. ISBN 0-3102000-8-3.

Richburg, Keith B. 1998. *Out of America: A Black Man Confronts Africa.* Harcourt Brace. ISBN 0-1560058-3-2.

Ricks, Annie. In press. *The True Story of a Teenage Black Girl.* Vantage Press.

Robbins, Anthony, and Joseph McClendon III. 1997. *Unlimited Power: A Black Choice.* S&S Fireside. ISBN 0-6848457-7-6.

Roberts, Bari-Ellen, and Jack E. White. 1998. *Roberts vs. Texaco: A True Story of Race and Corporate America.* Avon Books. ISBN 0-3809762-7-7.

Roberts, Paul Craig, and Lawrence Stratton. 1997. *The New Color Line: How Quotas and Privilege Destroy Democracy.* Regnery Publishing. ISBN 0-89526-423-4.

Roberts, Randy. 1999. *"But They Can't Beat Us": Oscar Robertson and the Crispus Attucks Tigers.* Sports Publishing. ISBN 1-5716725-7-5.

Robertson, David. 1999. *Denmark Vesey: The Buried History of America's Largest Slave Rebellion and the Man Who Led It.* Knopf. ISBN 0-79-44288-x.

Robeson, Paul. 1998. *Here I Stand.* Beacon Press. ISBN 0-8070644-5-9.

Robeson, Jr., Paul. 1993. *Paul Robeson, Jr. Speaks to America.* Rutgers University Press. ISBN 0-8135-1985-3.

————. n.d. *The Undiscovered Paul Robeson: The Early Years, 1898–1930*. John Wiley & Sons. ISBN 0-471-24265-9.

Robinson, Eugene. 1999. *Coal to Cream: A Black Man's Journey beyond Color to an Affirmation of Race*. Free Press. ISBN 0-684-85722-7.

Robinson, Rachel. 1998. *Jackie Robinson: An Intimate Portrait*. Abrams. ISBN 0-8109818-9-0.

Robinson, Randall. 1998. *Defending the Spirit: A Black Life in America*. Penguin USA. ISBN 0-525-94402-8.

————. 2000. *The Debt: What America Owes to Blacks*. Dutton/ Plume. ISBN 0-5259452-4-5.

Robinson, Sharon. 1996. *Stealing Home: An Intimate Family Portrait by the Daughter of Jackie Robinson*. HarperCollins. ISBN 0-06-017191-x.

Robinson, Wayne C. 1997. *The African-American Travel Guide*. Hunter Publishing. ISBN 1-5565079-7-6.

Roediger, David R., ed. 1999. *Black on White: Black Writers on What It Means to Be White*. Schocken Books. ISBN 0-8052-1114-4.

Rogers, Mary Beth. 1998. *Barbara Jordan: American Hero*. Bantam. ISBN 0-553-10603-1.

Rogin, Michael. 1998. *Blackface, White Noise: Jewish Immigrants in the Hollywood Melting Pot*. University of California. ISBN 0-5202138-0-7.

Roker, Al. 2000. *Stop This Car! Adventures in Fatherhood*. Scribner. ISBN 0-6848689-3-8.

Roses, Lorraine E., et al., eds. 1996. *Harlem's Glory: Black Women Writing, 1900–1950*. Harvard University Press. ISBN 0-6743726-7-9.

Ross, Jr., Lawrence C. 2001. *The Divine Nine: The History of African American Fraternities and Sororities*. Kensington Books. ISBN 1-5756663-4-0.

Rowan, Carl T. 1996. *The Coming Race War in America*. Little Brown. ISBN 0-3167598-0-5.

Rush, Sharon. 2000. *Loving across the Color Line: A White Adoptive Mother Learns about Race.* Rowman & Littlefield Publishers. ISBN 0-8476991-2-9.

Russ, Joanna. 1998. *What Are We Fighting For? Sex, Race, Class and the Future of Feminism.* St. Martin's Press. ISBN 0-312-15198-5.

Russell, Dick. 1998. *Black Genius and the American Experience.* Caroll & Graf. ISBN 0-7867-0455-1.

Rymer, Russ. 1998. *American Beach: A Saga of Race, Wealth and Memory.* HarperCollins. ISBN 0-06-017483-8.

St. Jean, Yanick, and Joe R. Feagin. 1998. *Double Burden: Black Women and Everyday Racism.* M.E. Sharpe. ISBN 1-56324-944-8.

Salley, Columbus. 1999. *The Black 100: A Ranking of the Most Influential African-Americans Past and Present.* Carol/Citadel. ISBN 0-8065204-8-5.

Salmond, John A. 1997. *My Mind Set on Freedom: A History of the Civil Rights Movement, 1954–1968.* Ivan R. Dee. ISBN 1-56663-140-8.

Saltzman, Jack, and Cornel West, eds. 1997. *Struggles in the Promised Land: Towards a History of Black-Jewish Relations in the United States.* Oxford University Press. ISBN 0-1950882-8-x.

Sandler, Stanley. 1998. *Segregated Skies: All-Black Combat Squadrons of World War II.* Smithsonian Institution Press. ISBN 1-5609891-7-3.

Sanjek, Roger. 1998. *The Future of Us All: Race and Neighborhood Politics in New York City.* Cornell University Press. ISBN 0-8014345-1-3.

Sartwell, Crispin. 1998. *Act Like You Know: African-American Autobiography and White Identity.* University of Chicago Press. ISBN 0-226-73526-5.

Scher, Richard K. 1997. *Politics in the New South: Republicanism, Race, and Leadership in the Twentieth Century.* M.E. Sharpe. ISBN 1-56324-848-4.

Schneider, Bart, ed. 1997. *Race: An Anthology in the First Person.* Random House. ISBN 0-517-70546-x.

Schubert, Frank W. 1997. *Black Valor: Buffalo Soldiers and the Medal of Honor, 1870–1898.* Scholarly Resource. ISBN 0-8420258-6-3.

Scott, Benjamin. In press. *The Assmilation of the White Man.* Vantage Press.

Scott, Daryl Michael. 1998. *Contempt and Pity: Social Policy and the Image of the Damaged Black Psyche, 1880–1996.* University of North Carolina Press. ISBN 0-8078463-5-x.

Senna, Danzy. 1999. *Caucasia.* Berkley Publishing Group. ISBN 1-5732271-6-1.

Shabazz, Attallah. In press. *From Mine Eyes.* Morrow/Avon.

Shakoor, Jordana Y. 1999. *Civil Rights Childhood.* University of Mississippi Press. ISBN 1-578-06192-x.

Sharpton, Al, and Anthony Walton. 1996. *Go and Tell Pharoah. The Autobiograpy of the Reverend Al Sharpton.* Doubleday. ISBN 0-3854758-3-7.

Shaw, Jr., Henry I., and Ralph W. Donnelly. n.d. *Blacks in the Marine Corps.* History & Museums Division, U.S. Marine Corps. L.C. call no. VE500.S5.

Shepard, Bruce R. 1996. *Deemed Unsuitable: Blacks from Oklahoma Move to the Canadian Prairies in Search of Equality in the Early 20th Century Only to Find Racism in Their New Home.* Pacific Pipeline. ISBN 0-6142536-5-9.

Sherman, Joan, ed. 1997. *The Black Bard of North Carolina: George Moses Horton and His Poetry.* University of North Carolina Press. ISBN 0-8078464-8-1.

Shields, David. 1999. *Black Planet: Facing Race During the NBA Season.* Crown. ISBN 0-6096045-2-x.

Shipler, David K. 1997. *A Country of Strangers: Blacks and Whites in America.* Knopf. ISBN 0-3945897-5-0.

Shipton, Alyn. 1999. *Groovin' High: The Life of Dizzy Gillespie.* Oxford University Press. ISBN 0-19-509132-9.

Shover, Michele, and Thomas Fleming. 1998. *Black Life in the Sacramento Valley 1850–1934.* Max Millard. ISBN 0-9631582-7-9.

Shropshire, Kenneth. 1996. *In Black and White: Race and Sports in America.* Foreword by Kellen Winslow. New York University Press. ISBN 0-8147-8016-4.

Sikora, Frank, Sheyann Webb, et al. 1997. *Selma, Lord, Selma: Girlhood Memories of the Civil Rights Days.* University of Alabama Press. ISBN 0-8173089-8-9.

Simms, Lois Averetta. 1995. *A Chalk and Chalkboard Career in Carolina.* Vantage Press. ISBN 0-5331139-0-3.

Simon, David, and Edward Burns. 1998. *The Corner: A Year in the Life of an Inner-City Neighborhood.* Broadway Books. ISBN 0-7679003-1-6.

Singletary, Mike, with Russ Pate. 1998. *Daddy's Home at Last: What It Takes for Dads to Put Families First.* Zondervan Publishing. ISBN 0-310-21569-2.

Sleeper, Jim. 1991. *The Closest of Strangers.* E.W. Norton. ISBN 0-393-30799-9.

———. 1997. *Liberal Racism.* Viking. ISBN 0-670-87391-8.

Slovo, Joe. 1997. *Slovo: The Unfinished Autobiography of ANC Leader Joe Slovo.* Foreword by Nelson Mandela. Ocean Press. ISBN 1-8752849-5-8.

Smiley, Tavis. 1996. *Hard Left: Straight Talk about the Wrongs of the Right.* Doubleday. ISBN 0-385-48404-6.

———. 2000. *Doing What's Right: How to Fight for What You Believe and Make a Difference.* Vantage Anchor Publishing. ISBN 0385499310.

Smith, Jessie Carney. 1996. *Powerful Black Women.* Visible Ink. ISBN 0-7876088-2-3.

Smith, John David. 1996. *Black Voices from Reconstruction, 1865-1877.* Millbrook Press. ISBN 1-5629458-3-1.

Smith, Robert C. 1996. *Racism in the Post-Civil Rights Era: Now You See It, Now You Don't.* State University of New York Press. ISBN 079142383.

———. 1996. *We Have No Leaders: African-Americans in the Post-Civil Rights Era.* State University of New York Press. ISBN 0-7914313-6-3.

Smith, Ronald L. 1997. *Cosby: The Life of a Comedy Legend.* Prometheus Books. ISBN 1-57392-126-2.

Smitherman, Geneva. 1996. *Educating African American Males: Detroit's Malcolm X Academy.* Third World Press. ISBN 0-88378-185-9.

Sniderman, Paul M., and Edward G. Carmines. 1997. *Reaching beyond Race.* Harvard University Press. ISBN 0-674-14578-x.

Sowell, Thomas. 1997. *Migrations and Cultures: A World View.* Basic Books. ISBN 0-4650458-9-8.

Speaks, Ruben L. n.d. *Church Administration from the A.M.E. Zion Perspective.* A.M.E. Zion Publishing House.

Spencer, Jon Michael. 2000. *The New Colored People: The Mixed-Race Movement in America.* New York University Press. ISBN 0-8147807-2-5.

Stanford, Karin L. 1997. *Beyond the Boundaries: Reverend Jesse Jackson in International Affairs.* State University of New York Press. ISBN 0-7914-3446-x.

Stanley, Leotha. 1995. *Be a Friend: The Story of African American Music in Song, Words and Pictures.* Zino Press. ISBN 1-5593315-3-4.

Staples, Brent. 1994. *Parallel Time: Growing Up in Black and White.* Pantheon. ISBN 0-679-42154-8.

Steele, Shelby. 1998. *A Dream Deferred: The Second Betrayal of Black Freedom in America.* HarperCollins. ISBN 0-0601682-3-4.

Steinhorn, Leonard, and Barbara Diggs-Brown. 1999. *By the Color of Our Skin*. New American Library. ISBN 0-5259435-9-5.

Stephens, Brooke. 1997. *Men We Cherish*. Doubleday. ISBN 0-3854853-2-8.

Sterling, Dorothy, ed. 1997. *We Are Your Sisters: Black Women in the Nineteenth Century*. Norton. ISBN 0-3933162-9-7.

Stewart, Jeffrey C. 1997. *1001 Things Everyone Should Know about African American History*. Doubleday. ISBN 0-3854857-6-x.

Stewart, Jeffrey C., ed. 1998. *Paul Robeson: Artist and Citizen*. Rutgers University Press. ISBN 0-8135251-1-x.

Stith, Anthony. 1997. *Breaking the Glass Ceiling: Racism in Corporate America: The Myth, the Reality and the Solutions*. Bryant & Dillon Publishers. ISBN 0-9638672-8-8.

Stotsky, Sandra. 1999. *Losing Our Language: How Multicultural Classroom Instruction Is Undermining Our Children's Ability to Read, Write and Reason*. Free Press. ISBN 0-6848496-1-5.

Stovall, Tyler. 1996. *Paris Noir: African-Americans in the City of Light*. Houghton Mifflin. ISBN 0-3956839-9-8.

Strege, John. 1997. *Tiger: A Biography of Tiger Woods*. Broadway Books. ISBN 0-553-06219-0.

Strugis, Ingrid. 1998. *The Nubian Wedding Book: Words and Rituals to Celebrate and Plan an African American Wedding*. Crown. ISBN 0-6098018-5-6.

Sudarkasa, Niara. 1996. *The Strength of Our Mothers: African and African American Women and Families: Essays and Speeches*. Africa World Press. ISBN 0-8654349-6-4.

Sullivan, Leon H. 1998. *Moving Mountains. The Principles and Purposes of Leon Sullivan*. Judson Press. ISBN 0-8170-1289-3.

Suskind, Ron. 1998. *A Hope in the Unseen: An American Odyssey from the Inner City to the Ivy League*. Broadway Books. ISBN 0-7679-0125-8.

Sutherland, Marcia. 1997. *Black Authenticity*. Third World Press. ISBN 0-88378-184-0.

Sutton, Ozell. n.d. *Civil Rights Legend: An Eyewitness to History.* Spectrum Communications Publishing Division. ISBN: None.

Tafari, I. Jabulani. n.d. *A Rastafari View of Marcus Mosiah Garvey.* Publisher unknown.

Talalay, Kathryn. 1997. *Composition in Black and White: The Life of Philippa Schuyler.* Oxford University Press. ISBN 0-1951139-3-4.

Talbott, Emma. 1996. *The Joy and Challenge of Raising African American Children.* Black Belt Press. ISBN 1-8813207-9-0.

Tallman, Edward. 1994. *Shaquille O'Neal.* Silver Burdett Ginn. ISBN 0-87518-637-8.

Tapper, Melbourne. 1998. *In the Blood: Sickle Cell Anemia and the Politics of Race.* University of Pennsylvania Press. ISBN 0-8122347-1-5.

Tate, Kimberly Cash. 1999. *More Christian Than African-American: An Autobiography of Spiritual Growth.* Rodale Press. ISBN 0-8759654-8-2.

Tate, Sonsyrea. 1998. *Little X: Growing Up in the Nation of Islam.* Harper San Francisco. ISBN 0-0625113-5-1.

Tatum, Beverly Daniel. 1997. *Why Are All the Black Kids Sitting Together in the Cafeteria? And Other Conversations about Race.* Basic Books. ISBN 0-465-09127-X.

Taulbert, Clifton. 1998. *Watching Our Crops Come In.* Viking Penguin. ISBN 0-1402443-4-4.

Taylor, Clarence. 1997. *Knocking at Our Own Door: Milton A. Galamison and the Struggle to Integrate NYC Schools.* Columbia University Press. ISBN 0-2311095-0-4.

Taylor, John E. In press. *The North Star.* Vantage Press.

Taylor, Quintard. 1999. *In Search of the Racial Frontier: African Americans in the American West, 1528–1990.* Norton. ISBN 0-3933188-9-3.

Taylor, Susan L. 1998. *Lessons in Living.* Doubleday. ISBN 0-3854837-9-1.

Taylor, Theodore. 1998. *The Flight of Jesse Leroy Brown.* Avon Books. ISBN 0-3809768-9-7.

Taylor, Yuval, ed. 1999. *I Was Born a Slave: An Anthology of Classic Slave Narratives.* Chicago Review Press, Inc. ISBN 1-5565233-1-9.

Terborg-Penn, Rosalyn. 1998. *African American Women in the Struggle for the Vote.* Indiana University Press. ISBN 0-2532117-6-x.

Thernstrom, Stephan, and Abigail Thernstrom. 1997. *America in Black and White: One Nation, Indivisible.* Simon & Schuster. ISBN 0-684-80933-8.

Thomas, Hugh. 1999. *The Slave Trade.* Simon & Schuster. ISBN 0-6848356-5-7.

Thomas, Velma Maia. 1997. *Lest We Forget: The Passage from Africa to Slavery and Emancipation.* Random House. ISBN 0-6096003-0-3.

Thompson, Julius E. 1993. *The Black Press in Mississippi, 1865–1985.* University Press of Florida. ISBN 0-8130-1174-4.

————. 1994. *Percy Greene and the Jackson Advocate: The Life and Times of a Radical Conservative Black Newspaperman, 1897–1977.* McFarland & Company. ISBN 0-7864001-5-3.

————. 1999. *Dudley Randall, Broadside Press, and the Black Arts Movement in Detroit 1960–1995.* McFarland & Company. ISBN 0-7864-0360-8.

Thornton, Yvonne S., with Jo Coudert. 1996. *The Ditchdigger's Daughters. A Black Family's Astonishing Success Story.* Dutton/Plume. ISBN 0-4522761-9-5.

Tiller, Ed. 1994. *Being a Black Republican—It's Not Easy.* Tiller Publishing. ISBN 0-961667-8-4.

Tinsley, Sonya. 1998. *Black Excellence.* Peter Pauper Press. ISBN 0-8808806-7-8.

Tosches, Nick. 2000. *The Devil and Sonny Liston.* Little Brown. ISBN 0-3168977-5-2.

Toussaint, Rose-Marie, and Anthony E. Santaniello. 1998. *Never Question the Miracle: A Surgeon's Story.* Ballantine/One World. ISBN 0-345-40723-7.

Trotter, Jr., Joe William. 1998. *River Jordan: African American Urban Life in the Ohio Valley.* University Press of Kentucky. ISBN 0-8131-2065-9.

Trotter, Jr., Joe William., and Eric Ledell Smith, eds. 1997. *African Americans in Pennsylvania: Shifting Historical Perspectives.* Penn State University Press. ISBN 0-271-01687-6.

Troupe, Quincy. 2000. *Miles and Me.* University of California Press. ISBN 0-5202162-4-5.

Trudeau, Noah Andre. 1998. *Like Men of War: Black Troops in the Civil War, 1862–1865.* Little Brown. ISBN 0-316-85325-9.

Turnbull, Walter, and Howard Manly. 1997. *Lift Every Voice: Expecting the Most and Getting the Best from All of God's Children.* Hyperion. ISBN 0-7868-8197-6.

Turner, Richard Brent. 1997. *Islam in the African-American Experience.* Indiana University Press. ISBN 0-253-33238-9.

Tusmith, Bonnie, ed. 1998. *Conversations With John Edgar Wideman.* University Press of Mississippi. ISBN 1-5780605-4-0.

Tygiel, Jules. 1998. *The Jackie Robinson Reader: Perspectives on an American Hero.* Dutton/Plume. ISBN 045227822.

Tyson, Timothy B. 1999. *Radio Free Dixie: Robert F. Williams and the Roots of Black Power.* University of North Carolina Press. ISBN 0-8078-2502-6.

Underwood, Bert. 1996. *A Study in Racism: USA.* Chester House Publishers. ISBN 0-935763-04-x.

University of Utah Press. 1997. *Black Pioneers: Images of the Back Experience on the North American Frontier.* Foreword by James L. Conyers Jr. University of Utah Press. ISBN 0-87480-546-5.

U.S. Marine Corps. n.d. *Montford Point. Camp Lejeune.* Campus Publishing Company, Inc.

Valis Hill, Constance. 2000. *Brotherhood in Rhythm: The Jazz Tap Dancing of the Nicholas Brothers.* Oxford University Press. ISBN 0-1951316-6-5.

Van Deburg, William L. 1996. *Modern Black Nationalism: From Marcus Garvey to Louis Farrakhan.* New York University Press. ISBN 0-8147878-8-6.

————. 1999. *Black Camelot: African-American Culture Heroes in Their Times, 1960–1980.* University of Chicago Press. ISBN 0-2268471-7-9.

van Sertima, Nobbles Cole, et al., contribs. 1996. *Infusion of African and African American Content in the School Curriculum.* Third World Press. ISBN0-88378-153-0.

Vanzant, Iyanla. 1996. *The Value in the Valley: A Black Woman's Guide through Life's Dilemmas.* Simon & Schuster. ISBN 0-6848247-5-2.

————. 1997. *Acts of Faith.* Simon & Schuster. ISBN 0-6848241-1-6.

————. 1997. *The Spirit of a Man: A Vision of Transformation for Black Men and the Women Who Love Them.* Harper San Francisco. ISBN 0-0625123-9-0.

————. 1998. *Faith in the Valley: Lessons for Women on the Journey to Peace.* Simon & Schuster. ISBN 0-6848504-8-6.

————. 1999. *One Day My Soul Just Opened Up: 40 Days and 40 Nights toward Spiritual Strength.* Simon & Schuster. ISBN 068483834.

————. 1999. *Yesterday, I Cried: Celebrating the Lessons of Living and Loving.* Simon & Schuster. ISBN 0-6848642-4-x.

————. 2000. *In the Meantime: Finding Yourself and the Love That You Want.* Simon & Schuster. ISBN 0-6848658-1-5.

Vibe Magazine. 1998. *Tupac Shakur.* Crown. ISBN 0-6098021-7-8.

Viteritti, Joseph P. 2000. *Choosing Equality: School Choice, the Constitution, and Civil Society.* Brookings Institution. ISBN 0-8157910-2-X.

Wachtel, Paul L. 1999. *Race in the Mind of America: Breaking the Vicious Circle Between Blacks and Whites.* Routledge. ISBN 0-415-92000-0.

Wade-Gayles, Gloria. 1995. *Pushed Back to Strength: A Black Woman' Journey Home.* Avon Books. ISBN 0-3807242-6-X.

———. 1997. *Father Songs: Testimonies by African-American Sons and Daughters.* Beacon Press. ISBN 0-8070-6214-6.

———. 1997. *Rooted against the Wind: Personal Essays.* Beacon Press. ISBN 0-8070093-9-3.

———, ed. 1996. *My Soul Is a Witness: African-American Women's Spirituality.* Beacon Press. ISBN 0-8070093-5-0.

Walker, Alice. 1996. *The Same River Twice: Honoring the Difficult.* Pocket Books. ISBN 0-671-00377-1.

Walker, Cassandra. 1997. *Stories from My Life.* Free Spirit Publishing. ISBN 1-5754201-6-3.

Walker, Clarence. 1996. *Breaking Strongholds in the African-American Family: Strategies for Spiritual Warfare.* Zondervan Publishing. ISBN 0-3102000-7-5.

Wallace, Howard L. 1996. *Federal Plantation: Affirmative Inaction within Our Federal Government.* Duncan & Duncan Publishers. ISBN 1-878647-24-5.

Waller, James. 1998. *Face to Face: The Changing State of Racism across America.* Perseus Publishing. ISBN 0-306-45865-9.

Wallis, Don. 1999. *All We Had Was Each Other: The Black Community of Madison, Indiana.* Indiana University Press. ISBN 0-2533342-8-4.

Walton, Anthony. 1997. *Mississippi: An American Journey.* Random House. ISBN 0-5171936-2-0.

Walton, Jr., Hanes. 1997. *African American Power and Politics.* Columbia University Press. ISBN 0-2311041-9-7.

Ward-Royster, Willa, with Tony Rose. 2000. *How I Got Over: Clara Ward and the World-Famous Ward Singers.* Temple University Press. ISBN 1-5663949-0-2.

Washington, Booker T. 2000. *Up from Slavery.* Lushena Books. ISBN 1-9300971-2-3.

Washington, Linn. 1998. *Black Judges on Justice.* New Press. ISBN 1-56584-437-8.

Watkins, Mel. 1998. *Dancing with Strangers: A Memoir.* Simon & Schuster. ISBN 0-6848086-4-1.

Watkins, S. Craig. 1998. *Representing Hip Hop Culture and the Production of Black Cinema.* University of Chicago Press. ISBN 0-2268748-8-5.

Watkins, Steve. 1997. *The Black O: Racism and Redemption in an American Corporate Empire.* University of Georgia Press. ISBN 0-8203-1916-3.

Wattleton, Faye. 1999. *Life on the Line.* Random House. ISBN 0-5174674-9-6.

Wedin, Carolyn. 1997. *Inheritors of the Spirit: Mary White Ovington and the Founding of the NAACP.* John Wiley. ISBN 0-471-16838-6.

Weinstein, Philip M. 1996. *What Else but Love: The Ordeal of Race in Faulkner and Morrison.* Columbia University Press. ISBN 0-2311027-6-3.

Weisenberger, Steven. 1998. *Modern Medea: A Family Story of Slavery and Child-Murder from the Old South.* FSG/Hill & Wang. ISBN 0-8090695-3-9.

Werner, Craig. 1999. *A Change Is Gonna Come: Music, Race and the Soul of America.* Plume. ISBN 0-452-28065-6.

Wesley, Charles H. 2000. *The History of Alpha Phi Alpha: A Development in College Life.* 17th printing. With an update by Robert L. Harris, Jr., and epilogue by Harry B. Dunbar. Foundation Publishers.

West, Cornel. 1993. *Race Matters.* Beacon Press. ISBN 0-8070-0918-0.

———. 2000. *The Cornel West Reader.* Basic Books. ISBN 0-4650911-0-5.

West, Cornel, and Kelvin Shawn Sealey, eds. 1997. *Restoring Hope: Conversations on the Future of Black America.* Beacon Press. ISBN 0-8070-0942-3.

Westheider, James E. 1999. *Fighting on Two Fronts: African Americans and the Vietnam War.* New York University Press. ISBN 0-8147932-4-x.

White, Armond. 1997. *Rebel for the Hell of It: Tupak Shakur's Art and Life.* Avalon New York. ISBN 1-5602512-2-0.

White, Constance. 1998. *Style Handbook for African-American Women.* Berkley Publishing Group. ISBN 0-3995237-9-0.

White, Deborah Gray. 1998. *Too Heavy a Load: Black Women in Defense of Themselves, 1894–1994.* Norton. ISBN 0-3930466-7-2.

White, Joyce. 1998. *Soul Food: Recipes and Reflections from African American Churches.* HarperCollins. ISBN 0-0601871-6-6.

White, Shane, and Graham White. 1999. *Stylin': African American Expressive Culture from Its Beginnings to the Zoot Suit.* Cornell University Press. ISBN 0-8014828-3-6.

White, Timothy. 1998. *Catch a Fire: The Life of Bob Marley.* Henry Holt. ISBN 0-8050600-9-x.

Whitman, T. Stephen. 1997. *The Price of Freedom: Slavery and Manumission in Baltimore and Early National Maryland.* University Press of Kentucky. ISBN 0-8131200-4-7.

Wicker, Tom. 1997. *Tragic Failure: Racial Integration in America.* HarperTrade. ISBN 0-6881556-0-x.

Wickham, DeWayne. 1997. *Thinking Black : Some of the Nation's Best Black Columnists Speak Their Minds.* Random House. ISBN 0-6098008-1-7.

Wideman, Daniel J., and Rohan B. Preston, eds. 1996. *Soulfires: Young Black Men on Love and Violence.* Penguin. ISBN 0-14-024215-5.

Wideman, John Edgar. 1996. *Fatheralong: A Meditation on Fathers and Sons, Race and Society.* Random House. ISBN 0-5171718-6-4.

Wiley, Ralph. 1996. *Dark Witness: When Black People Should Be Sacrificed (Again).* Ballantine/One World. ISBN 0-345-4005-0.

Wilkinson III, J. Harvie. 1997. *One Nation Indivisible: How Ethnic Separatism Threatens America.* Addison-Wesley. ISBN 0-201-18072-3.

Williams, Armstrong. 1995. *Beyond Blame: How We Can Succeed by Breaking the Dependency Barrier.* Free Press. ISBN 0-02-935365-3.

Williams, Donna Marie. 1997. *Black-Eyed Peas for the Soul: Tales to Strengthen the African American Spirit and Encourage the Heart.* Simon & Schuster. ISBN 0-6848374-5-5.

Williams, Gilbert Anthony. 1996. *The Christian Recorder, A.M.E. Church, 1854–1902.* McFarland & Company. ISBN 0-7864021-5-6.

Williams, Greg Alan. 1998. *Boys to Men.* Doubleday. ISBN 0-3854868-8-x.

Williams, Gregory Howard. 1996. *Life on the Color Line: The True Story of a White Boy Who Discovered He Was Black.* Dutton/Plume. ISBN 0-4522753-3-4.

Williams, Jason. 2001. *Loose Balls: Easy Money, Hard Fouls, Cheap Laughs and True Love in the N.B.A.* Broadway Books. ISBN 0-7679056-9-5.

Williams, Juan. 1998. *Thurgood Marshall.* Times Books. ISBN 0-8129-2028-7.

Williams, Lea E. 1996. *Servants of the People: The 1960s Legacy of African-American Leadership.* St. Martin's Press. ISBN 0-312-16372-x.

Williams, Lillian S. 2000. *Strangers in the Land of Paradise: Creation of an African Americn Community in Buffalo, New York, 1900–1940.* Indiana University Press. ISBN 0-2532140-8-4.

Williams, Lydia Frances. 1996. *Let's Go Git a Pint an' Be's Somebody: A Poetic Journey from Slavery to Forgiveness.* LFW Enterprises. ISBN 0-9648045-0-6.

Williams, Montel. 1997. *Mountain, Get Out of My Way.* Warner Books. ISBN 0-4466041-7-8.

Williams, Patricia. 1998. *Seeing a Color-Blind Future: The Paradox of Race.* Farrar, Straus & Giroux. ISBN 0-374-52533-1.

Williams, Willie L., with Bruce B. Henderson. 1996. *Taking Back Our Streets: Fighting Crime in America.* Simon & Schuster. ISBN 0-6848027-7-5.

Willis, Andre C., ed. 1996. *Faith of Our Fathers: African-American Men Reflect on Fatherhood.* Dutton. ISBN 0-525-94158-4.

Wilson, Sondra Kathryn, ed. 1999. *The Crisis Reader: Stories, Poetry and Essays From the N.A.A.C.P.'s Crisis Magazine.* Modern Library. ISBN 0-3757523-1-5.

Wilson, Sunnie, with John Cohassey. 1998. *Toast of the Town: The Life and Times of Sunnie Wilson.* Wayne State University Press. ISBN 0-8143269-5-1.

Wilson, William Julius. 1996. *When Work Disappears: The World of the New Urban Poor.* Knopf. ISBN 0-394-57935-6.

Wintz, Cary D., ed. 1996. *African-American Political Thought, 1890–1930: Washington, Du Bois, Garvey, and Randolph.* M.E. Sharpe. ISBN 1-56324-179-X.

Wirt, Frederick M. 1997. *"We Ain't What We Was": Civil Rights in the New South.* Duke University Press. ISBN 0-8223189-3-8.

Woideck, Carl. 1998. *The Charlie Parker Companion: Six Decades of Commentary.* Music Sales Corporation. ISBN 0-0286471-4-9.

Wood, Betty. 1998. *The Origins of American Slavery: Freedom and Bondage in the English Colonies.* FSG/Hill & Wang. ISBN 0-8090160-8-7.

Woodard, Komozi. 1999. *A Nation within a Nation: Amiri Baraka and Black Power Politics.* University of North Carolina Press. ISBN 0-8078246-1-5.

Woodard, Michael D. 1997. *Black Entrepreneurs in America: Stories of Struggle and Success.* Rutgers University Press. ISBN 0-8135-2368-0.

Woodson, Sr., Byron W. 2001. *A President in the Family: Thomas Jefferson, Sally Hemings, and Thomas Woodson.* Greenwood Publishing Group. ISBN 0-275-97174-0.

Woodson, Sr., Robert L. 1998. *The Triumphs of Joseph: How Today's Community Healers Are Reviving Our Streets and Neighborhoods.* Free Press. ISBN 0-6848274-2-5.

Woodward, Comer Vann. 1974. *The Strange Career of Jim Crow.* Oxford University Press. ISBN 0-1950180-5-2.

Wright, Bruce. 1993. *Black Robes, White Justice: Why Our Legal System Doesn't Work for Blacks.* Carol Publishing Group. ISBN 0-8184-0573-2.

————. 1996. *Black Justice in a White World: A Memoir.* Barricade. ISBN 1-56980-076-6.

Wright, Madeleine. 1998. *Sisters Helping Sisters.* African American Images. ISBN 0-9135435-3-5.

Wright, Richard. 1998. *Black Boy.* HarperCollins. ISBN 0-0609297-8-2.

Wyatt, Gail E. 1998. *Stolen Women: Reclaiming Our Sexuality, Taking Back Our Lives.* John Wiley. ISBN 0-4712971-7-8.

X, Malcom, with Alex Haley. 1999. *The Autobiography of Malcolm X.* Introduction by M. S. Handler. Epilogue by Alex Haley. (Reprint from African American Images, 1996.) Ballantine Publishing Group. ISBN 0-3459150-3-8.

ya Salaam, Kalamu. 1998. *The Magic of Juju: An Appreciation of the Black Arts Movement.* Third World Press. ISBN 0-88378-191-3.

Young, Andrea. 2000. *Lessons My Mother Taught Me.* Putnam Publishing Group. ISBN 1-5854200-7-7.

Young, Andrew. 1996. *An Easy Burden: The Civil Rights Movement and the Transformation of America.* HarperCollins. ISBN 0-06-017362-9.

Young, Robert. 1999. *The Emancipation Proclamation: Why Lincoln Really Freed the Slaves?* Silver Burdett Ginn. ISBN 0-87518-613-0.

Zafar, Rafia. 1997. *We Wear the Mask: African Americans Write American Literature, 1760–1870.* Columbia University Press. ISBN 0-2310809-5-6.

Zelnick, Bob. 1996. *Backfire: A Reporter's Look at Affirmative Action.* Regnery Publishing. ISBN 0-89526-455-2.

Zinn, Maxine Baca, and Bonnie T. Dill, eds. 1993. *Women of Color in U.S. Society.* Temple University Press. ISBN 1-5663910-5-9.

INDEX